Tales of an Itinerant Musician

by

Thomas W. Bailey, Jr.

The front cover and the caricature of Betty are by artist Hermeine Tovey. A talented artist and pianist, she has enjoyed a decade's long career in both mediums. The story "Pretzels and Pasties" in this book is the tale of one of our many adventures.

Table of Contents

FORWARD

When I share stories and anecdotes of growing up in a small town (not unlike the mythical one in the 1957 book Peyton Place), or of the people I have met and the experiences I have had as a professional musician, people say, "You have got to write a book." Where to start?

Since my adolescent years, I have kept a notebook in which I write things I want to recall days, weeks, months, years, and decades later. I began this practice in my high school English class. Our teacher, Betsy Jenrette, required us to keep a journal from which we were to complete essays for writing assignments. Already a working musician, I would write notes and blogs about incidents that I thought to be interesting, amusing, or disgusting. I would write about jokes I had heard, both fair and foul, and about people I encountered that I found to be, by societal standards, delightfully abnormal. To date, I have several composition books filled with this seemingly useless trivia. All of the stories are true. In a few instances, I have given those involved fictitious names in order to protect the innocent. Oh, wait—nobody was innocent.

A Character in Training

Growing up in a small southern town, I was no stranger to characters. The affable, colorful, interesting people who marched to their own drummers fascinated me. I have always been attracted to them and them to me. In my childhood, I never understood what it was that drew them to me like moths to a flame. It was in my teen years that the epiphany came. They gravitated toward me because I was one of them.

Always preferring the company of adults to my contemporaries, many an afternoon was spent eavesdropping on adult conversations. Tales of affairs, scandals, and long-buried secrets (all common in the south) kept my precocious imagination sated.

Our house was a haven for creative people. My mother, a professional musician and linguist, was a magnet for the artsy crowd. Their frequent visits brought me hours of joy. I loved hearing them talk and longed for a time when I would be old and worldly enough to have stories of my own.

"Aunt Sarah" was Mama's best friend. A soprano, she had studied at the Manhattan School of Music in New York City where she was a member of its Schola Cantorum. While in New York, she had performed onstage with Leonard Bernstein and Francois Poulenc conducting the New York

Philharmonic Orchestra. She and Mama often collaborated on musical endeavors.

"Uncle Kirk" was Mama's "brother from other parents." The educator, conductor, organist, and theater director kept me awestruck on his visits. An adventurous spirit, he was always on the go with one project or another and had wonderful stories of magical nights spent with larger-than-life people in the world of theater and music.

After his visits, whenever my sister, brother, and I saw a plane fly over, we would wonder if Uncle Kirk was on it, where he was going, what adventures he would have, and how long it would be before his next visit to tell us all about it.

Dr. Ann was a concert violinist who lived behind us. Mama helped her research, write her doctoral dissertation, and was her accompanist. When she came to our house to practice, my younger brother would hide. He had watched far too many 1930's and 40's Warner Brothers gangster movies on television and was convinced that the violin case with which she arrived contained not a musical instrument but a machine gun with which to kill us all. It was only after he heard the music of Beethoven or Mozart emanating from the living room that he would crawl out from under the bed or from behind the den sofa.

Our own family had its share of unconventional people, too. Hazel, an aunt by marriage, was the town Kleptomaniac. A nurse by profession, she met my uncle in

February of 1930. He was at the hospital visiting my Grandmother who had just given birth to my Father. They eloped the following Christmas Eve. The marriage took the family by surprise, as no one knew they had been dating. There was much family speculation about the secrecy of the courtship.

When nine months came and went without a visit from the stork, the shotgun wedding theory went out the window. Once they began living together, their differences in background became apparent. Divorce was unheard of in the south during that era so they remained together.

Her disorder manifested itself early in their marriage. The town merchants would notify my great-grandfather, the Chief of Police, when she stole from their stores. He or my uncle would pay for the purloined items and the incident would not be mentioned again.

As time went on, the thefts became more frequent and my uncle less tolerant. He would dutifully pay each shopkeeper for the lifted merchandise and then confront her. My uncle had been a heavy smoker of unfiltered Lucky Strike cigarettes since his teen years and suffered from emphysema. When agitated, he became short of breath. During his confrontations with Hazel, she would deny having taken anything. He would huff and puff and she would scream and curse. The encounters would end with him in his chair trying to catch his breath, she in the kitchen slamming pots and pans around, and nothing resolved.

On my mother's side of the family was a cousin who had resided in the state mental hospital since the late 1940's. She had fallen from a balance beam in a college gymnastics class, striking her head on the floor. She was never the same. Fancying herself a movie star, she wrote letters to her favorite celebrities: Greer Garson, Ingrid Bergman, Bette Davis, Hedy Lamarr, Judy Garland, and Joan Crawford were all recipients of the letters in which she would share with them her ideas about the films she would make with them. She would enclose a "publicity photo" of herself clad in a chartreuse one-piece bathing suit with matching high-heeled sandals. One of these notorious photographs hangs framed in my house.

When the stars received her letters, they reciprocated with autographed pictures of themselves with generic stock replies written on the backs. Desperate to be noticed by an agent (as if there were any in the small town in which she lived), she would stand on the platform at the depot, naked except for a red hat with matching shoes and purse waiting for the train with the talent scouts and agents from Hollywood. It was at this point that she was institutionalized. She remained a guest of the state until her 2008 death at age eighty-two.

Our family was blessed with a special friend who was with us for four generations. Miss Earline came into our lives in 1905 at the age of thirteen, to be a sitter and companion for my eldest uncle, then three years of age, while my great-grandmother gave birth to my middle uncle. She remained through my grandmother's birth in 1907 and became an integral part of the family. As she matured, she assumed the role of cook and housekeeper for my great-grandparents. In the 1920's, she was the third party in a love triangle, which ended in murder. Though she had a boyfriend, she also kept company with a married man. The two suitors became jealous of one another and fought over her. The married lover killed the boyfriend. Panic-stricken, Miss Earline helped the man hide the body. Each night for a week, they moved it from one location to another, placing it in bushes, under leaf piles, and in ditches until they could permanently dispose of it before it was discovered. All too soon, the crime was found out. Since Miss Earline was not involved in the actual killing (only an accessory after the fact), through the efforts of my great-grandfather–the police chief by whom she was employed–she received probation. Her lover went to prison for forty years.

She lived with my uncles and grandmother through their childhood. When my great-grandmother died in December of 1924, Miss Earline took over the household. In 1929, my grandparents married and their household was established, and Miss Earline cooked and cleaned for them. When my father was born in 1930, she embraced the opportunity to help rear a second generation. My parents married in 1958, and even though Miss Earline was now sixty-five years old, she decided that their house would be part of her domain, too.

She was there for my birth in 1960 and the subsequent arrivals of my sister and brother. Beginning to slow down, her domestic offerings were now limited to preparing the big, fancy Saturday lunch and special holiday feasts. Well into her eighties, her eyesight began to fail. While preparing her famous apple pie for the dessert at one of these meals, she had mistaken a can of black pepper for a similar can of cinnamon. Realizing her mistake, she attempted to correct the mishap by overcompensating with the cinnamon, adding about five times more than called for by the recipe. After lunch, Mama jokingly commented to her that the pie was spicier than usual and had a "little kick" to it. Taking it all in stride, Miss Earline replied, "Do Jesus, Miss Eleanor, I hoping ain't nobody gonna notice."

When I was young, I dumped a bucket of sand on her freshly mopped kitchen floor to build a sandcastle. I put salt into the sugar bowl on the kitchen table, rubbed buttery fingers on an antique satin bedspread, and committed other pranks that made extra work for her. I can still hear her distinctive voice saying, "Tommy Bailey, I gonna catch you and when I does, I gonna wahm yo' bawtm!"

Miss Earline was a big influence on our lives. She lived to see yet another generation with the birth of my sister's son. She died in the summer of 1983 at the age of ninety.

Pinewood school and St. Paul's Episcopal Church served as the foundation for the academic and spiritual education of my siblings and me. Here, the groundwork was laid for my musical education as well. Pinewood had several pianos and a home organ. St. Paul's had two pianos, a pipe organ, and a pump organ in the children's chapel. I seized every opportunity at school and church to try out my piano lesson pieces on all the various instruments. Each one had its own personality, like people.

Both school and church were nurturing environments. At St. Paul's, I sang in the junior choir. At school, I had many opportunities to play the piano. Pinewood was a unique place at which to matriculate. A private school founded in 1952, it was housed in an old mansion and its dependencies. We, as students, were encouraged to explore our own individualities. Classes were small and the student body and faculty diverse. There were boarding students from the Northeast as well as day students. The school offered extracurricular activities such as music lessons, horseback riding, afternoon study hall, and a summer camp and school in Keene Valley, New York. It was there in the summer of 1970 that I met one of my childhood nemeses who would become a mentor in my adolescence and a friend in adulthood. Dan Stone, now in his forty-sixth year on the faculty at Pinewood, was fresh out of college. I, a creative, strong-willed nine-and-a-half-year-old, and he a recent military college graduate, locked horns almost immediately. I was determined to do exactly as I pleased and he was equally determined that I do as I was told. The more authority he imposed upon me the more I rebelled. In situations where he was given the upper hand, all I had to do was throw up. He, being the grownup, had to clean both it and me up. This was our relationship for the rest of the summer; he'd badger, I'd barf. When school resumed after Labor Day for the 1970-71 school year, he was my fourth grade history teacher. Though we were friends by no means yet, at least the game of one-upmanship had ended. I liked his class. He made history come alive and took us on field trips. He encouraged my musical aspirations. When my grandmother would pull up at the school in her 1969 Ford to take me to my weekly piano lessons, he would gladly dismiss me from the obligatory after school P.E. class. To this day, I don't know if it was because he knew music would by my future or if it was because I was so inept at sports. Nevertheless, he was happy to have a break from me one afternoon a week.

All of those wonderful people, those larger-than-life characters who encouraged me, guided me, fought with me, and loved me during my formative years hold special places in my heart. Their stories were better than books or movies. The opportunities they gave me and the lessons they taught are more precious than Manhattan real estate. To the school and music teachers who encouraged me to be myself and develop my own unique talents, to those afternoon visitors who were master raconteurs, to my grandmother's friends who would insist I "play them a little tune," to my siblings who thought it was me and not our cousin who belonged in a mental hospital (but put up with me nonetheless), to my friends, colleagues, and students past and present who have told me repeatedly to put these stories into a book, I am grateful for the support. I am indebted to them for my ability to push beyond my comfort zone and succeed with my endeavors. I am grateful to have evolved into a character like those I admired in my youth.

Ghosts of Halloweens Past

Halloween in the late 1960's and early 1970's is a favorite memory from my childhood. Ideas for costumes began to be contemplated shortly after Labor Day. By October 1, the final wardrobe decisions had been made. Our mothers by now had met over cocktails comparing notes to ensure that there would be no duplication.

Several Halloween carnivals were held around town, hosted by the youth groups of local churches and by Pinewood School and The Summerville Academy, the two private schools in town. Bobbing for apples, costume contests, haunted houses, assorted games, fortunetellers, pony rides, and ghost stories were the order of the afternoon.

As the shadows lengthened, and the sun began its descent on the late October horizon, we headed home to prepare for the main event: Trick-or-Treating. Around 5:30 p.m., witches, ghosts, pirates, clowns, princes and princesses, action heroes, monsters, ghouls, goblins, vampires, gypsies, rock stars, spacemen, fairies, skeletons, mummies, aliens, nurses, Raggedy Ann and Andy dolls, comic book characters, and historical figures piled into sedans and paneled station wagons en masse to embark upon their annual quest for candy. We were dutifully admonished by our parents before ever leaving our respective driveways to be polite and thank the people for the candy. We were not to recite the obnoxious rhyme popular at the time:

"Trick-or-treat,

Smell my feet,

Give me something good to eat.

If you don't,

I don't care,

I'll pull down your underwear!"

With the precision of logistical engineers, our parents had houses and routes mapped out, complete with a timetable of who would be home when. Initial departure times were staggered so that the mechanism would work.

We children would spend ten to fifteen minutes at each house comparing and trading candy while our parents had a "quick cocktail". The evening would end around 8:30. The youngsters were bouncing off the walls from sugar overload and the adults were all drunk. Ah, the good old days!

The Francis Marion Hotel

During my childhood and early teen years, our family celebrations took place at the Francis Marion Hotel. It was named for General Francis Marion (nicknamed "The Swamp Fox" because of his ability to elude enemy troops and lead his men to safety by disappearing into the swamps) who was a hero of the Revolutionary War. Situated on the corner of King and Calhoun Streets, the hotel towers twelve stories above Marion Square, a public park once the parade ground for the original Citadel Military College. Welcoming its first guests in 1924, it was, at the time, the largest hotel in the Carolinas and among the grandest in the South. No trip downtown was complete without a stop at the venerable hostelry. If our morning had been spent shopping on King Street at the Condon's or Kerrison's department store or seeing an early movie at the Gloria or Riviera Theatre, our lunch destination was the hotel's Sugar and Spice Coffee Shop.

In the 1960's, my mother belonged to a duplicate bridge club that held its meetings on the mezzanine overlooking the grand lobby. We would accompany Mama to the hotel where we were joined by the children of the other club members. While the ladies waged war at the card table, we were entertained with organized activities. In that era, the hotel provided childcare services for its guests. The front desk kept a list of reputable, qualified sitters who could be hired by hotel patrons. One of the trips we took was to the Charleston Museum, a short walk up Calhoun Street at the corner of Rutledge Avenue. Another memorable excursion was a walk to the Battery at the foot of King Street. There, we would enjoy a picnic lunch prepared by the staff of the Sugar and Spice Restaurant. On tournament days (which began at 9am and ended at 4pm), we were taken on longer adventures. A boat ride over to Fort Sumter was one of our outings, but my favorite was a journey across town to Hampton Park. It is about a mile from the hotel and once had a petting zoo.

Our formal occasions were celebrated in the Swamp Fox Room. Our parents had gone there on many dates in mid-1950's and spent their wedding night at the hotel in June of 1958. My father would tell us about our family ties to the hotel and why coming there for special family celebrations were a continuation of a long tradition. His parents had held their wedding reception in the Gold Room in April of 1929, and his grandparents had attended the grand opening in 1924. He had feted many milestones in his youth at the hotel and wanted us to have the same experiences.

In my early teens, the Swamp Fox was a favorite destination. Not because of our family history, however—it was because of the piano that made its home in the restaurant. A large Baldwin grand, it had a thick glass top with an etching of Francis Marion in the center.

Around it, a ledge had been built and covered in leather. Bar stools with matching backs surrounded it. Patrons could sit at the piano for pre and post-dinner Cocktails while enjoying the music. George Creel, the pianist, was a friend of my parents. They had known him from other venues. By day, he worked for the South Carolina Employment Commission where his job was to help others find work. He moonlighted as a pianist. My father took me to hear him twice a month and I was fascinated by his ability to play the piano and carry on a conversation with guests at the same time. We would sit around the piano listening to him style popular songs as well as standards. He would sometimes tell ribald jokes to the regulars who would erupt into laughter and share one with him. Not wanting to appear unsophisticated, I would laugh too. When we got to the table, my father would explain to me what they meant. After our meal, we would return to the piano. George would ask me about my lessons and what I was playing and usually have me play for him while he smoked a cigarette. It was during these visits to George at the Baldwin that I first knew that the life of a hotel pianist was what I wanted my future—or at least part of my future—to hold. Securing my first restaurant piano job at the age of fifteen, my biweekly visits to George at the Francis Marion ended.

George moved to another hotel in the late 1970's, and I was in college playing several nights a week myself. He kept in touch with me and was always interested in what I was doing. I would have no occasion to be back at the Francis Marion until the summer of 1979. I was there for the graduation party of a friend and found myself bored with both the party and the company. For old time's sake, I decided to visit the Swamp Fox. Arriving at the entrance, the piano was no longer there. I was told that the restaurant and lounge were now two separate entities and the bar had been moved to the top floor. It was called The Top of the Marion, and the piano had moved with it. I took the elevator to the top floor. Its doors opened at the penthouse suite once occupied by General Mark Clark. Over in the corner of the living room, between two windows overlooking both King and Calhoun Streets, sat my old friend. Not many people were up there, so I sat down and began to play. After a few minutes, a man came over and introduced himself as Carl, the Food and Beverage Manager. He asked if I was looking for a job, explaining that the current pianist had given him his notice and would be leaving at the end of the month. Already playing elsewhere, I thanked him but declined the offer. I was intrigued by the possibility of playing there, but the timing was off.

Over the next few years, the hotel changed owners several times. Radisson bought it in the early 1980's and began renovations, which included moving the bar and the piano back into the lobby area. Now situated on the mezzanine, the piano was played daily during happy hour from 4pm until 7pm I was playing at the Sheraton Charleston Hotel on Lockwood Drive at the time, so there was no opportunity for me to play or even substitute at the piano that captured my heart a decade before. In September of 1989, Hurricane Hugo slammed into the eastern seaboard. Charleston bore the brunt of the storm. Much of the city was damaged. The hotel, though battered, survived. After about a year, it temporarily closed. There was much debate over what was to become of it. Many ideas were presented and rejected. Ultimately, it was decided that the icon of the city would reopen as the Francis Marion Hotel, just as it had always been, only better. Investors shared the vision of restoration and embraced the task with great enthusiasm. Once the project was complete, the hotel opened its doors again in 1996 and has been a vital part of the city since. Many of the original Art Deco features remain from the 1920's. The intricate wrought iron work in the lobby and stairs of the public areas has been painstakingly restored to its original splendor. The Swamp Fox Restaurant had been moved from its original location to the lower lobby. It now occupies the space, which, in former days, was the Sugar and Spice Coffee Shop. In my opinion, it was a wise decision. The old Swamp Fox Room was at the back of the hotel. To reach it, one entered the main lobby, ascended a flight of stairs to the mezzanine, turned right, went down a corridor, ascended two more steps, turned left, and went up another step to the restaurant. Unless one planned to be there and knew where it was, it was known only to hotel guests and locals. The new location, however, is ideal. With windows across the front, people passing on the sidewalk along King Street can see the welcoming, casual restaurant and bar. It is much more conducive to walk in guests and is handicap accessible. The hotel stays busy year-round with conventions, meetings, weddings, tour groups, banquets, reunions, and, of course, locals. It is even featured on the ghost tour that has two harmless spirits to add to the history and charm.

Since October of 2014, my dream of taking my place in the long line of musicians at the Charleston landmark has become a reality. I had been substituting for the regular pianist during his five-year tenure. When he decided to retire, the job was offered to me. At last, the stars had aligned. Both the job and the pianist were available at the same time.

The glass-topped Baldwin is no longer there; it disappeared sometime between 1989 and 1996. Perhaps it was sold, given away, damaged beyond repair during the hurricane, or even stolen. I have asked fellow musicians, local piano dealers, and even piano technicians about it. All of them recall the piano, but none of them knows where it ended up. Sadly, the piece of the hotel's history has been lost to the ages. I am on a mission to locate it or, at the very least, obtain a photograph of it for the hotel archives.

I don't know if the building actually has ghosts. However, I can sit in the lobby with my eyes closed and, in my mind, be momentarily transported back through the corridors of time. I experience ghosts of my own; my father, mother, and siblings are there. I can hear the lush chords and haunting melodies of George Creel at the Baldwin. I feel lucky and grateful to be playing there and hope to continue for many years to come, leaving my own imprint on the magical landmark while helping our guests create memories of their own.

The Big Apple

The telephone was ringing off the hook as I entered my apartment that June afternoon in 1981. With a bag full of groceries in one arm and a week's worth of dry-cleaning draped over the other, I rushed to answer it.

"Hi, sweetie, it's Nancie," came the voice of Nancie Purtill, one of the pianists with whom I shared the piano job in Albemarle's Restaurant in the new Sheraton Charleston Hotel.

"Are you busy?" she asked. I told her I had just come in, but if she'd hold the line long enough for me to close the door, I could chat.

"How would you like to play in New York?" she asked when I returned to the telephone. I thought she was joking.

"Oh, sure," I said, "tell the stage manager at Carnegie Hall to have a small Steinway in my dressing-room and a sixpack of Tab on ice."

"I'm serious; do you want to play in New York?"

"Well, sure, maybe one day when I'm older, good enough, and feel ready," I replied.

"Well, the offer isn't for some distant date in the next decade. It's for the second week of December this year, six months from now." I pondered the offer for about thirty seconds. I then told her I would love to but wasn't sure if I was good enough. Nancie was one of the few pianists in town whose opinion of me and my playing mattered. She had spent years in Manhattan playing in the biggest hotels and most fashionable restaurants and was a veteran of the Upper East Side cocktail party and reception circuit. While her primary employment had been the Waldorf Astoria Hotel in Peacock Alley and the Plaza Hotel's Palm Court, she had also been Kitty Carlisle's pianist of choice for functions both in her apartment and public venues. She had also been in demand as a reception pianist for various embassies.

"Honey," she said, "if I didn't think you could do it, we wouldn't be having this conversation. If every pianist playing in New York waited until they felt that they were good enough, there would be more vacant piano benches in Manhattan than occupied ones. I played there for ten years, worked all the time, and always felt that I was not ready."

"How did this come about? I don't know any New York pianists and I'm certain that none of them know me," I replied.

She explained that when she left New York three years before, she had passed her job in Peacock Alley along to a colleague and friend who had been a faithful substitute. In the time she had been in Charleston, she'd returned two or three times to substitute for him. He called and asked her to come up again in December. She declined due to other commitments on her calendar but had suggested me as a substitute for her. She had relayed to him that she and I were sharing a job and she thought it would be a great experience for me, both personally and professionally. He had gotten it cleared and the rest was up to me.

Over the next few weeks, we met often for coffee and planning sessions. I had spent the summers between 1970 and 1977 in upstate New York but had never been to New York City. I depended on Nancie to advise me. I knew how to buy an airline ticket but was unsure of where to stay, how to get around in the city, or where to eat. The logistical questions were endless, and she answered each one as I made careful and detailed notes.

There was a major hurdle to overcome; I needed a membership in the American Federation of Musicians. I had never joined. South Carolina, being a right-to-work state, did not have many unions. There was a chapter of AFM in Charleston, but it only had a handful of members. In order to work in the music industry in New York, one must belong to the AFM's Local 802. There were no exceptions. Upon investigation, we determined that joining the New York union was too costly for the four-day duration of the job. After a bit more research, we learned that one could join the Charleston chapter, receive a membership card issued by the national headquarters, and with that, be granted temporary work privileges as a visiting musician in other cities. The cost was minimal—problem solved!

The next item to check off my list was repertoire. The standards are a safe bet, and light classical pieces are good, but New York audiences, as explained to me, expect to hear songs from the current Broadway musicals. A phone call to Nancie's Manhattan colleague yielded a list of his twenty most requested songs. I knew all but two of them, and had six months to learn and commit them to memory.

Nancie told me that the piano in Peacock Alley, a 1916 Steinway, had belonged to Cole Porter, a longtime resident of the hotel. From that little bit of trivia, the idea was established in my head that I would be expected to play only the music of Cole Porter and whatever requests the hotel guest may have. For the remainder of the summer and well into the fall, I memorized as much Cole Porter music as I could.

In about the middle of November, I called Nancie to tell her that I was going to have to back out of the job. When she asked why, I told her that I only had an hour of Porter music memorized. I did not know enough of it to fill the three-hour time slot. When she stopped laughing, she asked where I had gotten the idea that I was only to play Porter songs. I told her that since she had made a point of telling me the history of the piano, I assumed that was what was required of the pianists who played it. She assured me that was not the case and I would be fine.

December came much more quickly than I would have liked. I was excited for the opportunity to play in New

York but at the same time was scared out of my wits. As I boarded the plane in Charleston that Sunday afternoon, I wondered what the next four days held for me. Best-case scenario, I would do a good job, see a little bit of the famous city, and be home Friday. The worst-case scenario was that I would be awful, make a complete fool of myself, be dismissed the first day, but still have three days to taste the riches of the Big Apple.

The nonstop flight from Charleston to New York's Laguardia Airport took two hours. The flight arrived late in the afternoon, just as darkness was falling over the city. The cab ride into Midtown Manhattan was worth the trip. The landmark buildings of the New York skyline were illuminated with hundreds of thousands of lights. When coupled with the city's Christmas lights, it was a feast for the eyes.

Once settled into my room at the Milford Plaza Hotel on 8th Avenue, I telephoned Nancie to let her know I had arrived. I then called Jimmy, her colleague for whom I was substituting.

The shift at the Waldorf was from 2:30 pm until 5:30 pm. This was the time of day when the hotel served high tea. Peacock Alley is located in the lobby directly across from the front desk. Next door is Sir Harry's, a more casual lounge. The area was not too crowded when I arrived shortly after 2 pm. I introduced myself to the manager, who showed me to the piano. The sixty-five year-old Steinway looked quite elegant in the setting. Its rich brown cabinet with carved scrolling wrapped around its legs, and its key desk had stenciling on its top and sides, complementing the equally ornate antique, freestanding clock just outside the room's entrance.

Relax, take a deep breath, I thought as I sat at the keyboard. For the first half hour, I played very familiar things while calming my nerves and getting accustomed to the instrument. Its action was a bit uneven and it was slightly out of tune, but that seemed to be par for the course with most hotel pianos.

The first set went very well—no requests, no complaints, a few compliments, and a couple of tips. The room got busier and noisier during the second set. This, while annoying to some performers, is always welcome with me. I feed on the energy in the room and become one with the environment. When the third and final set began, I was totally relaxed and confident. I was actually having a good time.

The teatime shift ended just as darkness was descending upon the city. I decided to save the cost of a cab and walk back to my hotel. I wanted to relax in my room for the first night because I had scheduled "touristy" things to do before and after work hours for the rest of my stay.

The easy forty-five minute walk between the two hotels, though chillier than I had anticipated, provided opportunities to see the city as it really was and not the way one would see it from the window of a tour bus. One can experience the sights, sounds, and smells much more intensely when immersed in them. I had never seen street vendors selling anything other than hotdogs, cold drinks, or shaved ice on the sidewalks of Charleston.

Even then, they were only seen in the summer. In New York, there was a different vendor every ten feet. T-shirts, umbrellas, souvenirs, and knock-offs, look-alike designer sunglasses, handbags, shoes, and perfumes could all be purchased from the sidewalk entrepreneurs. On less-traveled side streets and in alleyways, illegal substances and pleasures of the flesh could be had if the price was right.

Walking across Manhattan was like being on the set of a National Geographic television special. I encountered the faces of people of all nationalities and heard their languages and music. I could have stopped every few feet just to watch the diverse cultures.

My mornings were spent taking guided tours of various places around Manhattan by catching the earliest available buses. Most were three or four-hour tours that departed at 8am and ended around lunchtime.

I played the three hours at the Waldorf on Tuesday. It went as well as Monday had. A Chorus Line was in its sixth year and sold out most nights. I had a few requests for *One*, its big production number, and *What I Did for Love*, its torch song. There were also requests for songs from Annie. The patrons were friendly and generous tippers. I had not been asked to play anything I didn't know, and no one from management had come to the piano to tell me to play louder, softer, faster, or slower. They were not hovering over me telling me my music was too this or too that. So far, so good.

I had gotten advance tickets to Sugar Babies, which played at the Mark Hellinger Theatre on West 51st Street that evening. My shift ended at 5:30 pm and curtain time was not until 8pm, which allowed me two and a half hours for dinner. The famous Mama Leone's restaurant was on my list of places to go and was in the Theater District, so it seemed to be the logical choice. Once seated, my effervescent server gave me an encapsulated history of the place. With the encouragement and insistence of the great operatic tenor Enrico Caruso, Luisa Leone opened the first restaurant in her West 34th Street living room in 1906. Maestro Caruso filled the room to capacity with his friends, fans, and fellow musicians. As her name and fame grew, the restaurant moved to a bigger location. The current building boasted eleven dining rooms with a seating capacity of 1,250. The atmosphere of Italy was created with rococo statuary, plastic grapes, and strolling accordionists playing songs such as *O Sole Mio, Come Back to Sorrento,* and *Santa Lucia.* The food, though not five star cuisine, was good, and by Manhattan standards, inexpensive. Later at the theatre, Mickey Rooney and Ann Miller, at the ages of sixty-one and fifty-eight (respectively), sang and danced their way through their burlesque revival like twenty somethings. They were simply marvelous.

I had mentioned my walk from the Waldorf back to the Milford Plaza the previous evening to one of the servers in Peacock Alley. She told me what a dangerous and foolish thing I had done and added that I was lucky not to have been mugged .New York in the early eighties wasn't the Disneyland it is today. Heeding her advice, I had hailed a cab from the Waldorf to the restaurant, then from the restaurant to the theater, and finally from the theatre back to the Milford Plaza.

Wednesday and Thursday were spent shopping at Macy's and Lord and Taylor. I walked around Broadway taking pictures and being a typical tourist. Before I knew it, 5:30 pm on Thursday afternoon had arrived. I had completed the four three-hour substitute shifts at the famed Waldorf Astoria Hotel at 301 Park Avenue. In my final ten minutes at the piano, it occurred to me that no one had asked for, nor had I played any music by Cole Porter on his piano. I had planned to end with *"New York, New York,"* as I had on Monday, Tuesday, and Wednesday afternoons, but suddenly, the title of a Porter tune came to me. It seemed appropriate. After all, this entire experience had been a fluke: a lucky break for a young, green pianist who would not reach his twenty-first birthday for another nine days. I played *It Was Just One of Those Things* for its last line: *So goodbye, dear, and amen. Here's hoping we'll meet now and then. It was great fun, but it was just, just one of those things.*

Only in Charleston (Or in the Movies)

One summer early in my career, I was playing in the cocktail lounge of a smaller hotel. The venue was peculiar in its layout. The front desk, located in a petite lobby, was smaller than the foyers of the antebellum houses neighboring it. To the left of the front desk, one would ascend five stairs to reach the elevator to the restaurant and pool, a half story above the sidewalk. To the right of the desk, guests descended two steps to a corridor leading to the lounge, the public restrooms, and the door to the hotel parking lot, which was situated below street level. The lounge reminded me of the Adler and Ross song, *Hernando's Hideaway* from the Broadway musical The Pajama Game...*I know a dark secluded place, a place where no one knows your face, a glass of wine, a fast embrace. All you see are silhouettes and no one cares how late it gets...*

Though the year was 1980, the decor was stuck in 1960. A dim fluorescent light behind the bar, two enormous, illuminated tanks containing tropical fish and the round, dinner plate-sized windows in the swinging doors leading to the hotel kitchen provided the majority of the lighting for the room. There were banquettes covered in some type of velvet upholstery with tables, chairs, and barstools for seating. Each table had a candle housed in a ruby red glass holder which was encased in a white plastic faux lace, an ashtray and a book of matches bearing the name, address, and telephone number of the hotel.

In the corner of the room, its back facing the bar and its keyboard facing the wall, sat a sad-looking spinet piano that had seen its better days a decade before. Its wood finish was marred with water rings left by cocktail glasses and burn marks from cigarettes of previous patrons and pianists. Some of its ivory keys were chipped and the damper pedal squeaked intermittently, but all eighty-eight keys played. Though not at A440 pitch, it was at least in tune with itself.

It was from this little corner that I played Monday through Thursday evenings from eight until midnight. The clientele consisted of tourists, in for a quick nightcap after a long day of sightseeing and souvenir hunting, the flight crews of two major airlines that reserved blocks of rooms to accommodate overnight layovers, and, of course, locals. I have always loved playing for the locals. Those lovable barflies whose nightly arrivals and departures are accompanied by some sort of drama, which makes an average weeknight, take on a carnival-like atmosphere.

Sophia was one of the regulars. At five feet two inches tall and two hundred pounds, with the voice of a cartoon character and an icy stare that could exterminate lice, she made quite an impression upon those meeting her for the first time. She was no stranger to the bartenders and musicians around town nor did she fly under the radar of the local police.

In the early eighties, party drugs were all the rage in dance clubs. For those in the market for marijuana, cocaine, or angel dust, Sophia was the person with the connections. Most of her clients were people from out of town staying in the higher end hotels.

I was at the piano one Wednesday evening in June. It was about 9:30 pm and there were a dozen or so locals in the bar. Out of nowhere, Sophia appeared, out of breath from running and drenched in perspiration.

"Hide me, hide me!" She implored.

Her eyes darted frantically around the room searching for a place to conceal herself. Before I knew what was happening or had time to react, she had come behind the piano, gotten down on the floor between my legs, and was clutching my upper thighs for support and balance. Just then, the police came in asking if we had seen her. I glanced down at her as I continued to play.

"Don't say anything," she mouthed. We all feigned ignorance as to her whereabouts. Satisfied that she wasn't there, the officers left. Sophia remained behind the piano between my legs for another two or three minutes until she was confident that they were not coming back. Then, as abruptly as she had appeared, she hoisted herself up from her hideout and made a hasty exit through the same door by which she had entered ten minutes earlier. A few weeks later, she reappeared.

On the night in question, she had been carrying a pound of cocaine and several thousand dollars in cash in her purse.

Hookers, Harleys, and Hymns

I have been playing for funerals and memorial services in mortuary chapels for over thirty-five years. While some may consider this morbid, it does have its rewards. It is extremely gratifying to be able to supply music that is meaningful and comforting to the families and friends of the departed. Sometimes I play the organ and other times I play the piano or electric keyboard. There have been occasions when I have not played at all; I merely changed CDs on the sound system.

The term "mortuary musician" conjures images of an elderly lady or man seated at an equally ancient, electronic organ situated behind standing floral arrangements, playing softly in the background with the tremolo furiously wobbling. I am NOT that kind of organist. The musical taste of the deceased's family is the deciding factor in my choice of repertoire. I have played Bach, hymns, Broadway show tunes, contemporary Christian songs, country western ditties, rock and roll, and even jazz.

Over the years, I have played services in all sorts of environments. Some of the funeral homes are housed in beautiful southern mansions on tree-lined streets. Others are in buildings that resemble offices in industrial parks. The location does not seem to have any correlation to the behavior, or in some cases, the misbehavior of those for whom I am playing. Death can bring out the best or the worst in people. At the majority of services, the mourners conduct themselves with the dignity requisite of the occasion. These services all seem to run together in my mind. The ones in which people behave badly or, at the very least, inappropriately are the most memorable.

For the observer of human nature and those with an eye and an appreciation for the absurd, no better entertainment can be found than uncultured services. Those ones make the best stories. They require no embellishment or literary license. One could not fabricate anything more amusing than the reality of the occasions.

Some years ago in the early spring, I was engaged to provide music for the service of a prostitute who had been found dead from a drug overdose in a rundown motel room. The service was set for five o'clock in the afternoon. I arrived at the chapel about forty-five minutes prior in order to meet the funeral director as well as the police chaplain who was officiating. The consensus was that since the deceased had no particular religious affiliation, the most appropriate musical selections would be quiet, classical pieces. From the works of Johann Sebastian Bach, I chose *Arioso*, *Sheep May Safely Graze*, and *Air* from *Suite in D Major*. I followed these with *Largo* from *Xerxes* by Handel, *Theme* from *Finlandia* by Sibelius, and concluded with *Largo* from *The New World Symphony* by Dvorak.

Checking my watch and noting that it was about a minute until time for the service to commence, I looked out in the chapel to see if the chaplain and funeral director were in the back ready to begin. The sight my eyes beheld almost defies description. The room was about half full. With the exception of the family, every mourner was, in some way, connected to the sex industry. In attendance were other prostitutes, pole dancers, and pimps. All were dressed for work, ready to assume their positions on their respective street corners and in their strip clubs at the conclusion of the formalities. With the possible exception of a Fredericks of Hollywood catalog, I have never seen as many halter tops, fishnet stockings, platform shoes, large hoop earrings, faux gold chains, and polyester suits in one place.

Despite the solemnity of the occasion, it took every ounce of restraint I could muster not to play a medley of *Love for Sale, Let me Entertain You, Hey Big Spender, The Stripper,* and *Whatever Lola Wants, Lola Gets* as the assembly exited the chapel.

Another memorable service was for a member of the Hells Angels Motorcycle Club, the cause of death undisclosed. Rumors were abundant but were neither confirmed nor denied. As I approached the mortuary, I was greeted by well over one hundred bikers standing elbow-to-elbow in formation on the sidewalks on both sides of the street. The group was shaded by centuries old Live Oak trees dripping with Spanish moss, Harleys and Confederate flags at their sides. The formation continued into the chapel. Once inside, I was informed by the funeral director that aside from playing *Dixie* on the organ midway through the service, my duties would consist of operating the CD player before and after the service. Pink Floyd, Led Zeppelin, Alice Cooper, Styx, and Alabama were the bands whose recordings had been requested and provided by the family.

The only clergyman available to preside over the ceremony on this cold, gray, dreary January day was an elderly gentleman from a Pentecostal Holiness church. He had been apprised of the situation and instructed to keep the preaching to a minimum. About twenty minutes before the appointed hour of the service, I began to make my way from the office down the corridor to the chapel. With fear and trepidation, both my heart and mind were racing. I am an upper-middle class boy with a prep school, country club background in an expensive suit in the midst of this motley crew. As an outsider, I had to wonder if I would make it out alive. All of a sudden, I had an overwhelming urge to get the hell out of there. Professionalism is a trait for which I am well known. Bailing out twenty minutes prior to the service was not a viable option. If my general appearance and manner did not get me killed, abandoning these bikers in their hour of need certainly would. As I proceeded into the chapel and over to the CD player, I could feel the eyes of the bikers boring into me. What were they thinking? What would they do to me if one of the CDs wouldn't play? Where's the door?

My DJ duties went without mishap. No one was throwing things at me or pulling out switchblades. So far, so good. Several bikers eulogized. Their language was vulgar and their grammar appalling. The old parson read a few generic scripture passages at the conclusion of which I was to play *Dixie*. I had been instructed by the funeral director to play it two or three times considering its brevity. As I played, the pallbearers produced a bottle of Jack Daniels, which they passed amongst themselves, taking generous swigs directly from the bottle. My rendition of the song must have met their approval, because at its conclusion, someone yelled "Hell yeah!" and the assembly erupted into thunderous applause. The clergyman was visibly rattled but managed to keep his composure. Before ending the service by way of benediction, he admonished the crowd to "Seek the Lord" and "mend their ways".

On occasion, the funeral homes send me to play in churches. This happens when the resident musician is unavailable. Over the years, I have learned to adapt quickly to my surroundings. In the early years, however, I tried to avoid these situations. At the mortuary chapels, I knew the staff, the order of the services, the instruments, and the musical resources at my disposal. This is not the case when being sent to play in an unfamiliar church. Though most staff members at the host churches go out of their way to make guest musicians feel comfortable, there are times when questions arise that they simply cannot answer. When possible, I try to obtain from the family a list of hymns that are meaningful and comforting to them. I request permission to practice at the church the day before or early on, the day the service is to be held. I like to be familiar with the instrument I am meant to play. The size and condition of the instrument and the acoustics of the room all play a vital role in the way the music will sound.

On one of these occasions, I was called upon to travel to a little United Methodist Church in a small town about 35 miles from the city. I was told the church had a small pipe organ and a spinet piano. The family wanted the organ, but there would be a soloist who preferred to be accompanied by the piano. No problem. I would play the prelude, hymns, and postlude with the organ and play for the soloist at the piano.

It was agreed that I would arrive an hour and a half in advance to inspect the instruments, rehearse with the soloist, and begin the prelude half an hour prior to the appointed time of the service. The organ was a Moller with five ranks of pipes. It was in good repair and tune. I had just finished getting my music in order on the console when the soloist arrived. By way of introduction, she told me that her name was Esther and that she was the music teacher at the local elementary school and a volunteer choir director at the church. She said she played the piano well enough to know she should never do it in public. In her hand, she held two copies of "I Walked Today Where Jesus Walked" by Geoffrey O'Hara. Handing me a copy, she said it was one of her all-time favorites but she didn't have an opportunity to sing it very often because the church organist, a self-taught volunteer, couldn't play it.

As lovely as the little organ was, the piano left much to be desired. A Betsy Ross spinet model Lester, it probably had not been visited by a piano technician in several years. It qualified for what a pianist friend of mine calls a PSO–Piano Shaped Object.

Esther had a pleasant mezzo-soprano voice, good intonation, and an excellent sense of rhythm. I secretly wished she would allow me to accompany her with the organ but did not suggest it. I was afraid she might ask why, and I would have to express to her my opinion of the piano. For all I knew, she may have donated it to the church. A man in jeans and a faded, black T-shirt appeared in the back of the church as we concluded our rehearsal.

"Go home, Bubba. I can tell you are in no condition to work today," Esther told him. She explained that he was her brother. He had been shell shocked in the Vietnam War, was on disability, and was unemployable. He lived with her and did odd jobs around town when he wasn't at the VA hospital in the psychiatric ward. Though not officially on the church payroll, they let him sweep the sidewalks, empty trash cans, and cut the grass. For his services, he was payed twenty dollars in cash each week. He was supposed to use the money to help Esther with the groceries or utility bills, but more often than not, he would take it to the local convenience store and buy Colt 45 malt liquor or Boone's Farm Wild Mountain wine.

The service soon began. The congregation enthusiastically sang "Nearer my God to Thee" as the family and minister entered the sanctuary. An invocation was offered, followed by the recitation of the 23rd Psalm. I moved quietly to the piano. Esther rendered her solo beautifully. If anyone in the congregation noticed how badly out of tune the piano was, their facial expressions did not indicate it.

A local businessman was invited to the podium to deliver the eulogy. Clearly impressed by the sound of his own voice, the pompous, old windbag pontificated endlessly about the professional and civic accomplishments of the deceased. Esther glanced at her watch every two or three minutes and looked at me to roll her eyes. I began to detect quiet, nervous laughter. It was muffled, but it was laughter nonetheless. I looked at Esther. Her eyes were fixed on the back of the church. I turned on the piano bench to see what she was looking at. There stood Bubba, stark naked. Two ushers started toward the back of the church to escort him out, but Bubba began walking slowly up the center aisle.

"Naked came I out of my mother's womb, naked I shall return thither; the Lord gave and the Lord hath taken away; blessed be the name of the Lord. That's Job, Chapter One, Verse 21, King James Version," he said, then turned and walked out the door. Esther slipped out of the back door to find Bubba before the police did. I finished the service and drove back to Charleston.

People's behavior is not the only element that causes funerals to be memorable; I have played for many and have learned to expect the unexpected when working with family members on the music to be played. Perhaps the funniest was the service for an old maid named Gertrude. By all accounts, she was disliked by anyone who had the misfortune to make her acquaintance. She was described as being vindictive, bitter, demanding, and mean. Her only apparent redeeming quality was her love of animals. Having lived to the age of ninety-six most of her family and friends had predeceased her. She was survived by a niece and a nephew. Each had taken turns coming to Charleston on alternating weekends to tend to her affairs. One drove from North Carolina and the other from Georgia.

Prior to coming to the funeral home to plan her service, they had been at a meeting with her lawyer. It seemed that Gertrude had several million dollars in her estate. Her will directed that her house and its contents be sold. The proceeds from the sale were to be added to her portfolio. After her final expenses had been paid in full, her niece and nephew were to receive a check in the amount of $500 each and the bulk of the estate would go to various animal-related organizations.

When families offer that much-unsolicited information, we just listen. We let them vent and then continue guiding them through the service preparations. I asked what type of music they wanted.

The nephew said she was a devout Southern Baptist, so old gospel hymns like "How Great Thou Art" and "The Old Rugged Cross" seemed fitting. The niece was less charitable.

"As the casket is being rolled out of the chapel," she suggested, "I want you to play 'Ding, Dong the Witch is Dead' from *The Wizard of Oz*. Can you do that for me?" At the conclusion of the services, as per her wishes, I played the song. I did not play it in a rollicking, exuberant rendition as it was heard in the film, but instead in a rather stately, somber tempo reminiscent of a staid, German Lutheran chorale.

Betty

It was the summer of 1979, and I was playing piano during happy hour at The Mills House Hotel. On the job for only a week, I was already hearing tales of a notorious patron named Betty. The stories were numerous and told by hotel staff and clientele alike. She was a legend, but I had yet to make her acquaintance. This changed one sultry afternoon in June. She sauntered in around 5 pm, ensconced herself at a table for two next to the piano, lit a cigarette, and announced in the general direction of the cocktail waitress (who was taking an order from another table) that she'd have her "usual." Turning her attention to me, she asked, "Where is Dick and who might you be?"

I introduced myself and told her that Dick had moved over to the restaurant across the hotel and his new hours were 7 pm until 10 pm. Two hours, four single malt scotches, and a half package of cigarettes later, I had her entire life's story.

Born into a socially prominent Boston family in 1918, she had "escaped" the suffocating rules of New England society, much too conservative for her taste, by marrying an officer in the United States Navy. He hailed from an equally prominent family from Philadelphia's Main Line. She cared nothing at all for him, but he was her ticket out of Boston. She assumed that since World War II was raging, he would be shipped overseas and killed in action. She would collect his life insurance and widow's benefits and move to New York to launch a career as a commercial artist for New Yorker or Harper's Bazaar Magazine.

Life had not gone according to plan. Her husband returned from war unscathed. For the next twenty years, she dutifully played the role of the officer's wife. She had given birth to and reared two boys, ten years apart in age. She had been a Cub Scout den mother, a member of the ladies auxiliary at the VFW, baked cookies and cupcakes for Sunday school classes, and given elegant cocktail and dinner parties. By her sixtieth birthday, the conventionalism she had so desperately tried to escape in her youth had engulfed her completely. It was time for a change.

The previous winter, she had run away with a klezmer player she'd picked up at a Bar Mitzvah she crashed. They had a torrid sexual relationship in a seedy motel called The Siesta. The thirty-year age difference had been of little consequence to either of them. She proclaimed that she would still be with him, living in adulterous, orgasmic bliss, had her whereabouts not become known to her husband when the credit card bills started arriving.

She came in almost every afternoon and kept me entertained with stories of her life in Boston, Philadelphia, and New York in decades past. She was well read, well traveled, and had known many famous and interesting people. Whenever she suspected I didn't believe her, she would come in the following evening with letters, cards, or notes from the celebrity in question. She had attended parties with Tallulah Bankhead and Cole Porter in New York and had pictures to prove it. She knew the Gabor sisters and found Eva charming, Zsa Zsa insincere, and Magda crass.

She made the rounds to all of the venues with live music. Of everyone playing or singing in Charleston, she counted Andrea Dupree a talented young jazz singer, Hope Mustard a ballad and pop singer, and me among her favorites. She called us her "little lion cubs with golden manes". We were all tall, thin, young, and blonde.

Her visits continued for about a year. She would regale us with tales of her life, her miserable marriage, her trifling adult sons, and the mundaneness of her day-to-day existence. She declared that her afternoon and evening forays into the intoxicating world we musicians inhabit were like a zephyr on a hot, still afternoon or a cool oasis in the desert her life had become.

Without warning or explanation, the visits ended in the mid-autumn of 1980. No one knew what had become of her. After several weeks of no communication, a group of us went to her house to check on her. Upon arrival, we found the townhouse empty with a "For Rent" sign posted. Her former neighbor told us that her husband had died of cancer six weeks prior, and upon her return from Philadelphia where she buried him in his family plot, she had packed up and moved.

She had not told any of the neighbors where she was going or why. She had left no forwarding address with the post office, and her telephone had been disconnected. One of our regular happy hour customers worked for South Carolina Electric and Gas in the accounts receivable department. Although strictly against company policy, she looked to see if electric service had been transferred to another address. It had not.

As autumn gave way to winter, then winter to spring and finally to summer again, the question remained what had happened to our enigmatic Betty. Did she reconnect with the klezmer player? Was she living her dream of being a Bohemian artist in New York's Greenwich Village or Chelsea? Was she painting on the left bank in Paris, channeling the spirits of Monét and van Gogh?

Two years passed, and Betty was all but forgotten. There is a very high turnover among hotel and restaurant staff. Most of the people in the industry who knew, loved, hated, tolerated, or contended with her had moved to other jobs, other cities, or other social circles. Only we musicians remembered her, talked about her, and wondered if any of us would ever see her again.

By now, I had moved to a new hotel across town and was playing in its restaurant. One evening, about halfway through my shift, I saw a woman in the promenade (a long corridor that connected the main lobby to the restaurant, banquet and meeting rooms, lounge, and lobby level public restrooms) from the corner of my eye. There was a constant procession of people. As I continued to play, I could not help but think the woman looked oddly familiar. I could not place her. She continued to stand there and listen intently to the music. As quickly as the evening had begun, it was over. As I was gathering up my business cards, emptying my brandy snifter of tips, and restarting the piped-in music, I glanced back toward the promenade to catch a better glimpse of the mystery woman. She had vanished.

After making sure he didn't need me to wait around to give him a ride home, I bid our sommelier Franz a good night and exited the restaurant. The hostess told me that a woman had asked my name. When she found out, she asked what nights I played and what hours.

Jesus Christ, just what I need—a psychopath bag lady stalker, I muttered.

The piano in that establishment was placed toward the front of the room near the entrance and adjacent to the private dining room and wine cellar. Most of the tables were behind me and banquettes flanked the walls. I did not see her in the dimly lit back corner as I began my first set the following evening.

It wasn't until halfway through the second set that she appeared beside the piano.

"Tom, its Betty. It's been much too long. I've missed all of you and your music."

The woman standing beside me bore little resemblance to the Betty I had known two and a half—maybe three—years before. Gone was the elegant woman who wore Chanel tailored suits, genuine pearls and diamonds accessorized with Palizzio shoes and matching handbags. She was still tall and regal but rail thin and looked as though her apparel was composed of the spoils of a dumpster-diving excursion behind a thrift store. She was clad in a purple skirt, white blouse, Aigner shoes that had seen their better days, every piece of costume jewelry in Woolworth's inventory, and a patent leather clutch purse ten or more years out of style. Her hair, pulled back in a ponytail, accentuated her gaunt face. Unblended rouge was smeared across her high cheekbones, and she donned blue eyeshadow and lavender lipstick. She looked like Cruella de Vil in diminished circumstances.

I had a thousand questions to which she had a thousand answers, explanations, stories, fantasies, and lies which, over the course of the next ten years, she would reveal to us, burden us with, and baffle us by.

She quickly reestablished herself in the inner circles of Charleston's musicians' and artists' communities. Being very well read, she was very comfortable with writers. She had read everything that most people claim to have read but have not. She could discuss in great depth with the most learned professors of literature the intricate details of each work. Having been an art major in college, she had a working knowledge of all periods and styles of painting. She personally preferred painting with a palette knife rather than a brush. Music, though she did not play or sing herself, was her passion.

Her afternoon began around four. She would hold court at a corner table in a gay bar on King Street. She had the boys spellbound with her stories. They, in turn, would recount their sexcapades of the previous evening and would share with her their aspirations for the coming night's conquests. When they finished, she'd say, "Well, boys WILL be girls!"

For the next four or five hours, she would go from restaurant to bar to club, listening to her favorite musicians.

As her alcoholism progressed, her behavior became more outrageous, erratic, and entertaining. Seeing no sense in paying rent, she was evicted from more apartments in a year than most people occupy in a lifetime. One of her favorite tricks when she was out of money was to go into a bar and open a tab. She would have four or five cocktails, then ask the bartender to watch her purse while she went to the ladies' room. She then would sneak out, leaving behind an empty purse purchased for ten cents at a yard sale on the bar. The unsuspecting bartender was stuck with the tab. Later, when her annuity check arrived, she would go back and pay the tab, making an excuse that she had a personal emergency and had to leave.

She appeared toothless with the exception of her four eyeteeth. She had several explanations, none of which any of us believed. The first was that the landlord had come to collect the rent. She told him she wasn't going to pay; he punched her in the face, knocking out all but four of her teeth. Another story, more titillating but no less implausible, spun a tale of gum disease contracted from a Russian sailor she had a chance encounter with in the backseat of a taxicab.

Her friend Tony played piano at a restaurant on Meeting Street. At first, she was a great friend of the owners. They had given her a miniature poodle that she named after the restaurant in their honor. Her behavior in there was unbelievable. When she was drunk and they were busy, she would take it upon herself to "help" the hostess. Having been asked to stop, the last straw came one busy Friday evening. After consuming five single malt scotches, it was time to play "hostess" again. While the official hostess was seating a large party, Betty decided to seat a single man. He asked what the special was. Her reply was, "I don't know. Chicken or some goddamned thing, but they say it's good." As it happened, the man was a restaurant reviewer from the newspaper. Enraged, the owner ordered her off the premises, never to return.

Hurt and humiliated, she wasn't letting the incident go without exacting her revenge. She knew that the following Friday the restaurant had been bought out for the evening for a very large wedding rehearsal dinner. The guests were to arrive at 6pm. She calculated that the kitchen staff would arrive by noon to begin food preparations, and the doors would be unlocked for floral and linen deliveries.

She hired a taxi, went to the mall, and purchased fifty mice from the pet store. She then proceeded to call the health department from a pay telephone a block from the restaurant. Pretending to be an employee, she informed the health inspector that a large party was due later in the afternoon and the place was crawling with rats and roaches. She then had the cab take her to the alley behind the restaurant and wait until she entered through a side delivery door and released the army of mice. She then sat in the cab to watch the inspectors arrive and shut the place down.

In desperation for money to finance her growing alcohol and nicotine addiction, Betty began selling her jewelry at pawnshops. When she had exhausted that source of income, she decided to sell two Chippendale chairs which had been in her late husband's family since the 1700s and a painting by Charles Demuth (1883-1935) of Lancaster, Pennsylvania and Cape Cod, Massachusetts (a famed American artist she claimed to have been the sometimes-lover of her Uncle Bobby). Uncle Bobby had given her the painting as a wedding gift.

She met a man in a bar who had answered an advertisement she had placed in the newspaper. He represented himself to be an art and antiques appraiser.

Accompanying her to her apartment, she turned the chairs and painting over to him. He told her he would take them to the antiques auction in Atlanta where they would sell for top dollar. He would collect twenty percent commission and give her a check for the remaining eighty percent.

She never saw the man, the chairs, or the painting again.

Later that winter, she was evicted from yet another apartment. I received a phone call from her telling me the landlord had put all of her things on the sidewalk and that if I wanted anything to come get it. I have a beautiful china cabinet standing eight feet tall and a wood-inlaid cabinet in my house to this day that I salvaged from the sidewalk. She would accept no money for them or for any of the other items that her friends and neighbors carried away piece by piece that long ago winter day. She said things are not important. People are important.

A month later, catastrophe visited her again. I was awakened at 3am by a phone call. It was Franz from the restaurant telling me that "Ma Bett," as he called her, was in a crisis. She had fallen asleep on the sofa of her apartment with a lit cigarette and set the place ablaze. Her dog got out and ran away, and she made it out as well, but the apartment was a total loss. He said she was on a park bench a block away wrapped in a blanket with nothing but her purse. I drove into Charleston, picked her up, and brought her to my house where she stayed for two weeks.

During the time she was with me, she depleted my entire liquor supply and had the house in shambles. One night, after drinking herself into an alcohol-induced stupor, I took advantage of the opportunity of thoroughly cleaning the house. The following morning I awoke to find her gone. She left a note that read: ***"A house is meant to be lived in. This place is a damned museum. Thanks for everything. Betty."***

It would be ten months before I saw her again. I kept up with her via the musician's grapevine. I arrived at work one night in December to find a beautifully wrapped gift on the piano. Inside was a piano music box with a separate bench and a porcelain figurine of a girl in a brown dress sitting on the bench. There were smoke stains covering the piano and the figurine. Inside, in an area designated to keep jewelry and other trinkets, a note had been placed saying,

"Somehow, this survived the fire. The music box still works. Lift the piano lid and pull the spring up a little. Hope you enjoy it!
For Tom, Christmas Joy
Love Betty."

Now, thirty-some years later, that little piano, girl, and note are still in my music room.

Betty's gift to me. The figurine that survived the fire. Bailey collection

By the spring of 1986, my time at the hotel on the river had ended. The corporation had sold the property to a franchise, and live music was to be phased out. I had the opportunity to go to a new Italian restaurant on East Bay Street. Betty followed me.

At first, the staff didn't much care for her and regarded her as a nuisance. She was there most nights drunk. She had an ingratiating aura about her, and the owners, management, and staff quickly warmed up to her. By now, she was dressing in various shades of purple or magenta and wearing lots of dime store beads, rings, and earrings with wild hats and shoes. She dubbed this her "Decadent Mauve Period." She resembled the puppet Madame from the Wayland and Madame Television show. The likeness was so great that some of the waiters began calling her "Madame." She never knew that she was being made fun of. She thought they were being formal and found it charming. As she entered the bar, they would say, "Good evening, Madame. Will Madame be having her usual tonight?"

In other bars around town, the staff wasn't as kind. With only four eyeteeth, someone joked that she looked like Dracula's mother. Another replied that she looked like Dracula in drag.

At this point, she was drinking heavily and her antics were becoming more embarrassing than funny. Nancy Clayton-Lefter was playing at Marianne, a French restaurant on the corner of Meeting and Hasell Streets. She worked the 9pm to 1am shift in the piano bar in the back. She is a mezzo-soprano who can render a Handel aria with ease. She also possesses a popular voice not unlike that of Karen Carpenter. I would frequently stop in between my gigs for a late supper to enjoy her vocal stylings. One evening, I came in around 10pm only to find Betty. Atop the grand piano was a synthesizer, and below was an octave of pedals connected to a drum machine. Betty—clearly in a foul mood—drummed her fingers, green from the metal bands of the dime store rings, on top of the piano.

"Dull, dull, dull," she muttered. Looking directly at me, she said, "Take me home."

I told her that I had just gotten there, that I was out with friends to unwind after work, and that I wasn't planning to leave any time soon.

"Then advance me cab fare," she demanded. I told her that I was going to settle my bill with a credit card and had no cash with me. She erupted into a rage that came out of nowhere, like sheet lightning.

"Goddammit!" She shouted as she slammed her cocktail glass down onto the piano, spilling its contents. She stormed out of the restaurant, screaming something about if anything happened to her on her way home it would be on our collective conscience. The drink quickly spread, making its way across the piano and coming dangerously close to the synthesizer. We all pitched in, sopping it up as best we could in a valiant effort to prevent Nancy from being electrocuted. Ever the professional, she continued to sing and play until the song ended. We just looked at each other in disbelief, wondering what had just happened.

By now, we were all veterans of such drunken scenes and their aftermaths. No one was surprised when we didn't see Betty again for several months. This was her modus operandi: create a public spectacle and then pull a disappearing act. Eventually, she made her grand re-entry but was not received as warmly as she had been in the past. We were all becoming weary of the drama she created and the embarrassment she caused on our jobs. I was cordial but distant.

Already extremely thin, she had lost a significant amount of weight. Her clothes hung on her. Somewhere along the way, she had acquired a set of false teeth which were entirely too large for her mouth. If she looked like

Dracula's mother or Dracula in drag before, she now looked like the sister of Mr. Ed, the talking horse. None of us could imagine why she had bothered to get dentures at this late date. She lived on scotch and cigarettes. She would take long drags on her Virginia Slims, inhaling deeply. No smoke ever came back out. Where it went eluded everyone who witnessed it. She drifted from place to place for the rest of the summer but never really reconnected with anyone for any length of time. I was to see her one final time in early December of 1992. It was a chance encounter on the sidewalk along Liberty Street. She said she was going to move to the beach as soon as she could find a place. She was stooped and frail with an ashen complexion. I could not help feeling sorry for her.

Betty, 1938 – Bailey collection

The following May, a death notice appeared in the newspaper. There was no obituary. A few weeks later, I bumped into Sparky, a local cab driver. He said he had been transporting her from the beach back to the city several times a week for appointments at the Navy Hospital. He was not charging her for the cab rides. She never disclosed to him the nature of her illness, and when he asked how she was feeling, she would tell him she was fine and quickly change the subject. He suspected that she had an advanced stage of cancer. He said when the end came; it was he who had discovered her body. Arriving to take her to an appointment and getting no answer at the door, he called the Folly Beach Police who opened the door to her one-room studio apartment where her body was found on a folding beach chaise lounge, the only furniture in the room. She had been dead for about twenty-four hours.

There was no funeral. Her eldest son had her cremated and carried her ashes around in a canvas tote bag. He, too, disappeared about eighteen months later.

Rumors circulated that he had not reported her death to the Navy or to Social Security and continued to collect both checks and deposit them into their joint account. When the fraud was discovered, he fled in the middle of the night, leaving everything in his Section Eight apartment behind.

In addition to the china and crystal cabinets, I have the little music box, a couple of books, some photographs, and a portrait Betty painted of me. I think of her often and fondly. All of the older musicians in Charleston, of which I am now one, still tell Betty stories at parties and on our jobs. She lives on.

Betty's portrait of me. Done with palette knife.

Bailey collection

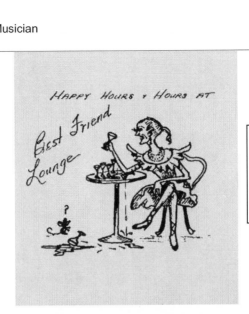

Hermeine Tovey's caricature of Betty

Bailey collection

Tom and Betty listening to Hope Mustard
Bailey collection

Typical Betty

Bailey collection

A young visitor at the piano.

Bailey collection

Backstage at the Gaillard Auditorium
Bailey collection

Strange Encounters

Mr. Shoe Laces

While depositing coins in a parking meter one crisp, autumn afternoon, I was approached by a scruffy looking young man. He did not give the appearance of being hungry or homeless, just in need of soap and shampoo.

"Excuse me, sir; can you do me a favor?"

Expecting him to ask for money, a cigarette, or a ride somewhere, I thought I had an answer to whatever he was about to ask. I don't carry cash or smoke and I had just parked the car and couldn't drive him anywhere.

"I'll try," I said.

He continued, "I tie people's shoes for them for a living. My business is really starting to take off. I have even been approved for an ad in the yellow pages. Will you help me spread the word?"

"Sure," I said, mentally rolling my eyes.

"Thank you sir and God bless you," he replied as he continued down the sidewalk.

Wrong Number

I was walking into a rehearsal when my cellphone rang. There was no name on the screen but it was a local number so I answered it.

Me: Hello?

Caller: Are you at home?

Me: No, I am walking into a meeting.

Caller: I need some toilet paper, Donald. I am in the bathroom and I'm totally out.

Me: I think you have the wrong number.

Caller: Is this Donald?

Me: No.

Caller: Where's Donald?

Me: The only Donald I have ever known was a classmate my freshman year in high school. That was 1975. I have not seen him in forty years.

Caller: You bring me some toilet paper, then.

Me: I have no idea who you are or where you live. Besides, I am about to be late for my meeting.

Caller: Please don't do this to me; I'm begging you.

Me: Do what to you?

Caller: Are you dense? Leave me sitting here with no toilet paper.

Me: Lady, you have the wrong number. I would like to help you but I can't. I'm sorry.

Caller: You're selfish, and I'm cutting you out of my will!

And with that proclamation, she slammed the phone down.

Are You a Lawyer?

Walking down Market Street on my way to work, a middle-aged woman in a form-fitting, one-piece, leopard print shorts outfit, gold flat sandals, and pink tinted sunglasses approached me. In a heavy, Bronx-type accent, she asked, "Ah ya a loya? Ya kinda look like a loya in ya coat and tie in this heat."

I assured her I was not a lawyer but if she needed one, Broad Street is lawyer row.

"Oh no, I just thawt ya were a loya 'cause ya kinda look like one." She seemed disappointed that I wasn't an attorney. I did not tell her that I was a musician on my way to work in the hotel directly in front of her. I didn't want her hanging around in there.

As she continued down the sidewalk, she stopped another middle-aged man and asked, "Ah ya a dahkta? Ya kinda look like a dahkta."

As I crossed the street and walked into the hotel, I wondered if she was a "hooka". She kind of looked, dressed, and acted like one.

Palm Beach Lady

While playing a happy hour piano job, a woman came and sat down at a table next to me. She closed her eyes and swayed in time to the music. About every other song, she told me I was the best pianist she had ever heard and she could listen to me all afternoon. A few songs later, she reported that she thinks she is supposed to be meeting her husband here, but can't be sure because last weekend, while drunk, she fell and hit her head and has a concussion so she could very well be imagining the whole thing. I just smiled and continued to play.

I played, she swayed.
She then relayed that she was just passing through town from her winter home in Palm Beach to her summer place in Maine.

I played, she swayed.
She asked me if I had ever played in Florida. I told her that I had performed as both a pianist and organist in Jacksonville, St. Augustine, Palm Coast, Bunnell, and Miami. She said that Donald Trump lived across the street from her in Palm Beach and that she could get me hired to play at all of his parties but not to expect much. She said she went to all of his parties and he served bottom shelf liquor and frozen Hors D'Oeuvres from Costco.

I played some more, she swayed some more.
I had to close my eyes while I played because her incessant swaying was making me seasick.

She asked what my favorite piece to play was. I told her and she requested that I play it for her. As I began, she abruptly stood and told me her husband had obviously stood her up and that she was leaving. She told me I played beautifully and that she'd call Donald when she got to Maine. She said she'd have him call me, but I was under no circumstances to tell him that she had no plans to vote for him. With that, she went on her merry way.

Perfume or Cologne

I was standing on a street corner waiting for the traffic signal to change. A woman demanded of me, "Good God, what is that VILE perfume you're wearing?"

"It's not perfume, its cologne," I answer. "It's called Aramis, it costs eighty dollars a bottle, and I've been wearing it for thirty-five years."

"Well," she said, "it smells like a dog's ass."

"I wouldn't know, ma'am," I said. "I don't make a habit of smelling dogs' rear ends. Have a nice day."

I crossed the street before the light changed to avoid any further conversation with her.

Thank You (I Think)

I once played weekends at a small inn. It was actually two buildings joined together by an enclosed breezeway that served as a hallway connecting the inn with the restaurant and bar. It also housed the restrooms. In the center, against the wall, was a large, old, upright piano that could be heard in both the lobby and restaurant. It was painted the same color as the walls.

As I was playing, a man on his way to the facilities stopped and said, "Oh, you're real. I thought it was recorded music." He then disappeared behind the men's room door, leaving me to ponder the meaning of what he had just said. On one hand, he could have meant that the music was so pleasant, mistake-free, and unobtrusive that it seemed to be a recording. On the other hand, could he have been suggesting that it was so uninteresting and soporific that it seemed to be "elevator music"? Shortly, he emerged from the lavatory and plopped a twenty-dollar bill on the piano.

"Play on, young man," he said, returning to the restaurant.

On another occasion, at the same venue, a couple appeared beside the piano. I had been playing a medley of Andrew Lloyd Webber songs that had been requested by some other patrons. I had gotten most of the songs from *Phantom of the Opera*, *Cats*, *Evita*, and *Song and Dance* checked off the request list and was about to play *Starlight Express* when the woman said, "The music of Andrew Lloyd Webber is eminently forgettable, but you play it very well."

Not knowing how to respond, I said, "Thank you… I think."

Napkin Nibbler

I was playing one evening in one of the lounges in a downtown hotel when a woman who looked to be in her late fifties or early sixties, came in and seated herself on the leather sofa directly in front of the piano. Making herself comfortable, she ordered a Manhattan. When it arrived, she took a sip, sniffed her underarm, and nibbled on her paper cocktail napkin. Her pattern of sip, sniff, and nibble went on for about twenty minutes until both the cocktail and the napkin had been consumed. She ordered another cocktail and something from the tapas menu. The ritual began again: sip, sniff, nibble. I took a two-minute break and told the cocktail waitress and bartender what I was observing. They thought I was making it up, but each walked by her and saw for themselves what I had already told them.

From the piano, I could see both the woman and the lounge staff who were stationed behind her. They were all doubled over trying to be discreet in their laughter. By now, napkin woman had consumed two more Manhattans and two more napkins. She had the cocktail waitress remove the untouched tapas tray and told her that she would be glad to pay for it but wasn't going to eat it after all. Ordering a fourth Manhattan, she began the sip, sniff, and nibble routine once again. I could stand it no longer; I felt that I must underscore this strange scene with appropriate music.

When she sipped, I played a little of the Rodgers and Hart song, *Manhattan*. When she nibbled, I would slip in a bit of *The Lonely Goat* from The Sound of Music. No songs about underarms immediately came to mind until suddenly, as though through divine inspiration, it came to me: The jingle from the old television commercial for Shower-to-Shower deodorant powder. My medley went like this:

"We'll take Manhattan and Staten Island too,
It's lovely going through the zoo,
High on a hill was a lonely goat
Singing a sprinkle a day helps keep odor away
Have you had your sprinkle today?"

The lounge staff was in hysterics, and the woman was totally oblivious as to what was going on. She ordered a fifth Manhattan to take up to her room. As she staggered toward the elevators, the bartender suggested calling housekeeping and having them deliver an extra roll of toilet paper to her room in case she got hungry during the night.

Cafe Francais

I was sitting in the pleasant courtyard of a French pastry shop one afternoon. A lady came out with her coffee and pastry and sat at a table opposite me. She reminded me of the "Church Lady" character from Saturday Night Live. She wore a two-piece blue suit with a matching pillbox hat. In a carrier, which resembled a designer handbag, was an adorable teacup poodle. Being an animal lover, I commented on the dog and told her about my two fur children.

She introduced herself as Lucille from Mobile, Alabama. I asked how she happened to settle in Charleston. She said a combination of circumstances occurring simultaneously had helped her make the decision to relocate. Hurricane Katrina had devastated the coasts of Alabama, Mississippi, and Louisiana, leaving her neighborhood in ruins. Her long-time gentleman companion had died of a massive heart attack the week following the storm. She said they had been together for nearly twenty years but had little in common other than their mutual love of animals and unquenchable desire for physical gratification when they both were younger. They met at an animal rescue facility where they both volunteered. They never cohabitated but visited back and forth regularly.

When he died, he left her his house, a substantial life insurance policy, and his bank accounts. He had no family. She sold his condominium and what was left of her property and had used the proceeds to finance her move and buy a modest townhouse.

I suggested that she let her little companion out of the carrier to explore the fenced courtyard. We resumed our conversation while the dog explored every inch of the area. On the fence was a large mural of a Parisian sidewalk cafe. Its bright colors seemed to intrigue the dog. It looked at the people in the painting as if expecting them to drop a crumb. I asked Lucille what the dog's name was. She said she had named her "Brassiere." My curiosity was peaked so I asked how she came up with such an unusual name. Her reply was much more cogent than I had anticipated. "Well," she said, "She is a French breed, and a French dog should have a French name. ' Brassiere' is the only French word I know how to spell without looking it up."

Want to Buy a Duck?

For the past four decades, Charleston has hosted SEWE (Southeastern Wildlife Exposition). Held annually in February, it is a four-day festival dedicated to all things wild. Art shows feature the works of artists and craftsmen, whose subjects range from forest animals to birds and fish. Chefs offer samples of freshly prepared wild game, and vendors who cater to hunters and fishermen set up tents and booths displaying and offering for sale their goods and services. The festival is attended by thousands of people from across the south.

Charlestonians have never needed an occasion to throw a party, but the expo in town is as good a reason as any. I vividly recall one such affair in the early 1980's. Asked to provide piano music for a celebration given in honor of a famed wildlife artist, I arrived at the South Battery, home of one of the city's most prominent hostesses.

Though not one of the artists whose work would be presented that year, Mr. John Henry Dick, who specialized in capturing the images of mallard ducks on canvas, was the guest of honor. I had done some research before the party, discovered that he was also a published author, and worked on various projects and publications for the Audubon Society.

When I arrived, I was shown in by the caterer and presented to the hostess. We needed no formal introduction; I had played for her in the past.

It was unusually cold in Charleston, the temperature hovering at freezing. Both the hostess and the artist had been sipping hot buttered rum all afternoon to "warm their bones." Neither were feeling any pain.

Inside the mahogany-paneled drawing room where Mr. Dick was seated by the open fire in a leather wingback chair, he nursed his drink and awaited the arrival of the party guests.

Says she in her inebriated state, "Mr. Bailey, may I present my dear friend and celebrated artist for whom this party is being given, Mr. John Henry Duck. He paints dicks exquisitely!"

The Heart of Charleston

In its heyday, the lounge at the Heart of Charleston Motel, located at 200 Meeting Street, was the place to be. It was a small lounge with a seating capacity of about twenty-five people. Hidden from the street on the backside of the office and check-in desk and facing the raised pool situated in the middle of a horseshoe driveway, it was one of Charleston's better-kept secrets. The two-story motel was built in 1960 on the footprint of The Charleston Hotel (1839-1959) which had closed a year earlier. It was typical of motor court architecture of its day with brick veneer, iron railings, and concrete walkways.

The tiny lounge, equally unremarkable and originally intended for motel guests, had evolved into a local hotspot. Some considered it a private club.

Marie, the evening bartender, was the attraction. She was a unique woman with an uncanny ability of accurately assessing the character of a person in under a minute. She had an expansive vocabulary and a repertoire of expressions as colorful as the rainbow flags flying in San Francisco's Castro District. Her clientele was quite eclectic; they could easily have been characters from a Tennessee Williams play or a Damon Runyon novel. Moguls rubbed elbows with misfits, lawyers drank with Lotharios, and dowagers exchanged pleasantries with ditch-diggers. A visit to the

Heart was never dull. If there were no drama naturally occurring, someone would create it.

"Gin Jane" (as Marie called her due to her propensity to drink gin and tonic) occupied a seat at the end of the bar next to the glass door leading to the front desk. She complained bitterly about everyone and everything and missed no opportunity to expound upon the glories of her home state of Ohio.

Colleen, another regular, was usually drunk when she arrived. Her libation of choice was piña colada. The more she drank, the more morose she became. She told the same story, day after day, of how much in love she was with a married man. She kept the books for his construction company free of charge and was at his disposal to satisfy the needs his wife would not, yet he refused to obtain a divorce and marry her. She would cry until her mascara had run all the way down her face and her large, false eyelashes were floating in the cocktail.

"Colleen," Marie would say, "if you don't stop that crying, I'm going to slap you and give you something to cry for."

Bobby and Gabrielle were an unlikely pair who stopped in every afternoon. Gabrielle was a refugee from Germany. Having come to Charleston in the 1940's to escape the ravages of World War II, she had worked as a secretary at a local hospital and was the sole beneficiary of the estate of her longtime roommate. The estate was left in trust and administered by an attorney from whom she received a monthly allowance to supplement her social security. She wore the same outfit every day. A T-shirt with the slogan "I Love New York" was paired with Bermuda shorts and a pair of silver house slippers accented with plastic jewels.

Bobby, twenty years her junior, wore baggy chinos, tennis shoes, and a filthy, white, long-sleeved dress shirt missing the cuff buttons. Afflicted with neurofibromatosis, he had lumps and knots on his arms, hands, neck, and face.

Bobby would order a Pilsner beer for her and a Diet Coke for himself. They would spread travel brochures out on their table and discuss each destination in detail, making plans for trips they would never take. Gabrielle nursed the beer, but Bobby guzzled the Diet Coke because refills were free. After he drank four or five, Marie would inform him she was running a bar, not a soda fountain. Indignant, he would hastily gather up their brochures, mutter something about never coming back, and escort Gabrielle out. The next afternoon, they would be back.

John and Scotty, two middle-aged, alcoholic lawyers, didn't miss a day. If the place was open, they were there. Seated at the bar in their dark suits and straw fedoras, they passed their afternoons reliving long-resolved cases and congratulating themselves on their courtroom prowess.

Lillian, a woman who gave the appearance of being homeless, would come in once or twice a week. She drank beer and filled Marie in on what the other bartenders were up to. Tourists, mistaking her for someone down on her luck, would often try to give her a five or ten dollar bill. She would laugh at them and pull a $100 bill from her bra with which to settle her bar tab.

One night, she was leaving at the same time I was. Marie asked me to drop her off at her apartment because she was too inebriated to walk the five blocks. I loaded her into my 1977 Toyota Corolla and set off into the night. When we arrived at her apartment, she refused to get out of the car. She was convinced I had taken her to the wrong address. After almost thirty minutes of trying in vain to reason with her and running out of ideas, I noticed that several days of mail was falling out of the mailbox on her porch. I grabbed a piece of it and brought it to the car, showing her that her name was on it and therefore it *was* her home. Satisfied, she got out of the car and went inside without so much as a thank you. When I got home, I discovered that she had urinated in the passenger seat. That was the first and last time I ever drove her anywhere.

Fred and Phil were longtime best friends who had dubious reputations all over town. Both were successful business owners. They arrived at their offices between 6:30 and 7am every day and worked until noon. They would meet for lunch and then go to an early afternoon Alcoholics Anonymous meeting. After the meeting, they spent the rest of the afternoon drinking. One afternoon, they decided to walk two blocks over to a restaurant on Market Street. Both had been drinking martinis for about two hours. On their walk, they were stopped by a police officer who noticed that Phil was walking with one foot on the sidewalk and the other in the gutter. The officer asked if everything was all right. Phil said they were fine and asked why the officer thought otherwise. The police officer explained that he had noticed that he'd been walking with one foot on the sidewalk and the other in the gutter for more than a block.

"I am glad you told me," said Phil, "I thought I'd had a stroke. God Bless you, officer."

Vivian was a regular when she wasn't in the state mental hospital for evaluation. If anyone dared call her crazy or in any way suggested her mental state was a little precarious, she would inform them she had three sets of papers from the mental institution declaring her fit to walk the streets. She would then ask them if they could say the same. One afternoon, she burst through the door screaming.

"They killed my babies! They killed my babies!"

" What are you carrying on about, Vivian? You don't have any children. You've never even been married," Marie replied.

"They killed my babies! They killed every one of them," she repeated. She then grabbed an ashtray from a table and smashed it against the wall of the bar. Running back out of the door, she jumped, fully clothed, into the pool. Knowing that she couldn't swim, Marie dispatched a few bar patrons to rescue her. Once out of the pool, she was taken to the ladies' room and given towels to dry off. After about thirty minutes, Marie realized Vivian had not returned. Concerned, she went to check on her. In the ladies' room, she discovered Vivian naked on her hands and knees in a stall washing her clothes in the toilet.

"Darlin', if I were you, I'd hold onto them good and tight when you run them through the rinse cycle or they'll go right on down!" Marie advised in disbelief.

The police came and transported Vivian back to the mental hospital for another evaluation. She would return three months later with a fourth set of papers confirming her sanity.

Louie, the security guard of the motel, was the ne'er-do-well black sheep of a prominent family. He looked like the Barney Rubble character from The Flintstones cartoon, only with black hair.

He spent most of his working hours hiding to avoid working and drinking vodka from bottles, he kept stashed in the shrubbery around the motel property. To mask the odor of alcohol on his breath, he chewed cloves of garlic. Marie frequently told him that he was safe from vampires. He was seldom seen without the stump of an unlit cigar tucked in the right corner of his mouth. Always harassing lounge patrons, he had been nicknamed "Deputy Dog".

One December, Marie asked him what he wanted for Christmas. He thought for a moment and said what he wanted most was a little female companionship on Christmas Eve. There were no takers. No woman in a hundred-mile radius would entertain the idea, not even "working girls." Not wanting to disappoint him, Marie decided the only thing to do was to get him an inflatable love doll. A collection was taken up among the lounge regulars. When the price of the doll had been collected, a procurement team was sent to an adult novelty shop to make the purchase. After the lounge closed on December twenty-third, we all pitched in to get Louie's date ready. We inflated her with a bicycle pump, dressed her in a Kmart negligee, and put two strands of Mardi Gras beads, one red and one green, around her neck. Marie hid her in the bar supply closet. Just before the lounge closed at 4pm the afternoon of Christmas Eve, Louie was presented with his gift. Already drunk, he was delighted. He loaded his latex lover into the basket of his bicycle, and went careening down the street toward his apartment.

The day after Christmas, we all piled into the lounge and eagerly anticipated a report from him on his night of passion. He finally appeared. He said when he got home; he carried her into the apartment and poured himself a tall glass of vodka. When he was feeling relaxed, he joined her on the couch. She looked beautiful in the soft light. He said he put his arms around her and kissed her cheek. Next, he tried to nibble on her neck. He said she obviously didn't like that, because when he did, she hissed at him and flew across the room, landing in the corner.

Little Mary, as we called her, dropped in about once a month. While small in stature, her character was larger than life. No one knew much about her or where or if she worked. She walked everywhere, so we all assumed that she lived downtown. A quiet person, though not rude or aloof, she would speak when spoken to but never initiate a conversation. We suspected she had a phobia of germs. She refused to drink from a bar glass and thought that plastic was "peasantly." When ordering her scotch straight up, she insisted it be served in the ceramic mug she kept in her purse. She would sit alone at a corner table and write on a yellow legal pad for hours at a time. No one knew what she was writing. Whenever anyone came near her table, she would close the tablet. When asked if she was working on the next bestselling novel, or perhaps a plot to overthrow the government, she would look up at the person posing the question, smile, and reply, "Could be." By the end of the evening, having consumed two or three mugs of straight scotch, she paid her tab, removed a hammer from her large purse, and left. She said the hammer was for protection, and if anyone tried to mug or molest her on her walk home, they would be very sorry.

The biggest kook of them all was Edward. Standing nearly seven feet tall and weighing about 175 pounds, he made quite an entrance. No one knew exactly how old he was. His age varied depending on what kind of mood he was in. Sometimes he was almost "forty." Other times, he was "seventy and holding up quite well." He was one of the people the local musicians referred to as "The Rock People." We only saw them once a month around the full moon. We imagined them slithering out from under and behind rocks, stalking the city one night a month. They would return home before the sun came up, not to be seen or heard from for another thirty days.

Edward had held many jobs and by his own admission had been let go from all of them. He claimed that his ideas were too innovative for the average employer who couldn't quite seem to share his vision. At times, he would appear as the captain of a yacht in white slacks and a blue blazer. Other times, his attire was bizarre. Once, he came in wearing a neon yellow rain slicker and a combat helmet, carrying a large police flashlight. Shining the light first in the faces and then the laps of lounge patrons, he would say "Ve have vays of making you talk." On these occasions, we did not know if he thought he was the Gloucester Fisherman or Colonel Klink from Hogan's Heroes.

His constant companion was a stuffed pig named Thurmond that he carried around in a Gucci tote bag. Edward spoke through Thurmond. If something was not to his liking, he would complain but say it was Thurmond doing the complaining.

He came up to me on a job one night while I was playing a request.

"You must stop playing that song at once," he commanded. "Thurmond despises that song."

I told him to tell Thurmond that the song was a request and I had been given a generous tip for playing it. He went back to his bar stool to relay the message. Within thirty seconds, he was back at the piano. He said that Thurmond did not care that it was a request or how much some tourist had paid me to play it. If I didn't stop, he was coming over and leaving his hoof prints on my forehead.

"You tell that swine if he kicks me," I threatened, "I am going to have bacon for breakfast and a ham sandwich for lunch tomorrow."

"We don't like you," Edward snapped as he walked out of the restaurant. I accompanied his departure with music from *The Three Little Pigs*.

Al was another character. He was employed by the Medical University to begin converting records to electronic storage and troubleshoot their computer systems. He lived in a room at the motel and spent all of his off-hours in the bar. Chain-smoking Marlboros and downing vodka and soda like water, he quickly became tiresome. He was one of those people who could bore you talking about you. If he ever bathed, it was no more than once a month. His hair had enough grease in it to fry three chickens. He either only had one outfit—black pants and a white turtleneck—or several sets of identical shirts and pants which he wore year-round. The turtlenecks always had a brownish tinge to them. When asked, he explained that coin laundries were too expensive, so he hand-washed his clothes in the lavatory of his room in Listerine. This undoubtedly explained the medicinal scent combined with his body odor.

Betty was no stranger, either. She stopped in every evening for a nightcap after already visiting several other bars since midafternoon. One evening, she hobbled in on a walking cane and said she had twisted her foot on the uneven sidewalk on her street. Seated at the bar was a woman named Grace who was the hostess at the neighboring restaurant. Betty did not particularly care for her, and the feeling was mutual. The feud started when Grace, at the request of her boss, had asked Betty, who was drunk and making a scene, to leave. Betty left but said nasty things about Grace, her employer, and the restaurant all over town. On this particular evening Betty was swilling down Drambuie. After six liqueurs and an hour of trading barbs with Grace, she decided to say goodnight. Standing, she got the walking cane tangled with the leg of the barstool and fell backwards into a large potted palm. Marie rushed to her aid. Once she was back on her feet, Grace quipped, "If you can't hold your booze, then don't drink so much."

Betty replied, "I'm not drunk, you witch. I can't manage this cane. It's all about the leverage."

"Sure it is, you old sot," Grace grumbled.
Not ready to allow her to have the last word, Betty retorted, "You should call it a night too, dearie. You wouldn't want to get a ticket. I saw your broom when I came in and it's double-parked."

The motel closed in 1990, thus ending an era. Bank of America bought the entire block and erected a building that housed a branch of the bank and corporate offices for the company's subsidiaries. Marie went to work for the Days Inn a block down the street. She stayed there until 1995 when she retired. Some of the old gang followed her, but it never had the spirit of our beloved, old watering hole.

Gin Jane moved to Ohio, never to be heard from again. Colleen finally gave up on her married lover and returned to her home state of Texas. Marie gets a card from her every Christmas. Gabrielle, Lillian, John, Scotty, Fred, Phil, Vivian, Louie, Betty, and Grace all died. Bobby moved to Tennessee and severed all ties to Charleston. Edward and

Little Mary are still around and make cameo appearances once or twice a year. Marie and I are in our thirty-eighth year of friendship. We talk on the phone several times a week and see each other about once a month. She is now in her late 70's and doesn't get out at night much anymore. She hosts holiday parties at her house. Those of us who remain eagerly attend to sip wine or White Russians and reminisce about the golden era of The Heart.

Publicity photo – 1982
Bailey collection

TOM BAILEY

Directing a production at Garrett High School.
Bailey collection

*Gary Collins, Tom, and
Mary Anne Mobley (Miss
America, 1959) at the March of
Dimes Telethon.*

Bailey collection

With Mary Ann Mobley at the March of Dimes, Telethon.

Bailey collection

A Tune for a Tyrant

Once in the city by the sea, I played in a nice hotel restaurant situated on a river. It was the newest luxury hotel in town and therefore attracted discerning travelers and locals who enjoyed being seen at the trendiest new places. At first, I shared the job with two other pianists; Nancie Purtill played Monday through Wednesday nights, Ralph Wise played Thursday through Saturday nights, and I covered the Friday business lunch and the Sunday brunch. Ralph left after about a year. Nancie took his Thursday through Saturday nights, I picked up her Monday through Wednesday schedule, the Friday brunch was dropped, and we alternated weeks playing Sundays. This arrangement worked well for about eighteen months. Nancie was a great friend and mentor from whom I learned much. When her husband's job took them to another state, I inherited the entire schedule, playing seven days a week.

The restaurant staff was like a big family. Going to work at night was fun because we were all together. As anyone who has ever worked in the hospitality industry can attest, middle management changes quickly, often, and without warning. Our beloved food and beverage director was transferred to a newer, larger venue and was replaced with a horrid man who happened to be from the Middle East. Within a week, he was both hated and feared by the entire restaurant and lounge staff. He found fault with everything. If he saw an improperly folded napkin, a piece of silverware out of place, or a salt shaker that was only partially filled, he would grab the end of the tablecloth and jerk the entire table setting onto the floor, often shattering china and glassware. Woe to the server whose station the table was in. Often, he would creep around corners trying to catch staff socializing on the clock or not working. If caught, the offenses were grounds for termination.

I was answerable to the general manager of the hotel, not him. He was not happy about the fact that he had no authority over me, but there was nothing he could do about it. The staff took advantage of this by making me the official "lookout". From my vantage point at the piano, I had a clear view of the dining room entrances from both the kitchen and the hallway. It was decided that a secret signal should be established between the piano and the staff to alert when "The Sheik," as they called him, was on the prowl. It was to be a piece of music very distinctive, yet one not likely to be requested by clients (lest there be any false alarms). His Middle Eastern heritage being his defining attribute, we decided to choose a song characteristic of that region. We had brainstorming sessions after work over cocktails for several evenings in an attempt to find the perfect piece without him suspecting. Some suggestions were *The Sheik of Araby, Theme From Lawrence of Arabia, Abdul, Abulbul Amir,"* *Ahad the A-rab*, and select themes from

Scheherazade, but all seemed too obvious. Finally, we settled upon *Misirlou,* a Greek/Turkish folk melody which had been made into a 1940's popular song. By the 1980's, it was seldom heard, no one ever requested it, and it had the Arabic flair we were seeking. We began using it immediately, sometimes two or three times a night. The wait staff nicknamed it *Music to Screw Camels By.* It worked like a charm for the duration of his tyrannical tenure.

Fast-forward twenty years. It was the spring of 2005 and I was playing at Charleston Chops, a high-end steak house in the heart of the historic district. About halfway through the evening, a server delivered a twenty dollar tip accompanied with a note that read, "Please play *Music to Screw Camels By.* It took me a minute to put it all together in my head before the memories came flooding back. My eyes immediately began searching the restaurant to locate the author of the note. Our eyes met. It was Clayton, one of my coworkers from long ago. He raised his wine glass to me. When my shift ended, he and his travel companion joined me at the bar where we drank wine, reminiscing about our time together. He reminded me of the one and only run-in I had with "The Shiek." Every night when I came in to work, there was a ratty-looking, dust-laden silk floral arrangement on the back of the piano. I would move it onto the floor by the piano and leave it there at the end of the night. The next night, it would be back on the piano, and I'd put it back on the floor. This continued for about a week. One evening when I arrived, The "Shiek" was in the restaurant, which was already half full of patrons. The arrangement was on the piano and I moved it to the floor as usual. He bolted over, picked up the arrangement, and slammed it down on the back of the piano.

Yelling at me, he declared, "I want this to stay on the piano! Don't move it again!" There was a fire in his jet black eyes. My own blue eyes saw red. I continued to play with my left hand, and with my right, backhanded the arrangement off the piano onto the floor, yelling back at him.

"I'm not playing with that weed in my face!"

He stormed off. The arrangement was never on the piano again.

Pretzels and Pasties

The weeks between Thanksgiving and New Year's Eve are one of the busiest periods in the world of the working musician. In addition to our regular playing engagements, there are many holiday parties, weddings, and school and church programs, which require our services. On the rare occasion that we have a night off (or, at the very least, an early evening), we, like most other professionals, like to relax and unwind. Such was the case on a mid-December evening in 1986.

My good friend and fellow pianist Hermeine Tovey and I were playing holiday parties at opposite ends of the same hotel, both of which ended at 10 pm. We had talked about doing something after work but had not made a firm commitment to anything. Both of us, feeling adventurous, decided to use this opportunity to broaden our horizons a little. Neither of us had ever been to a strip club and decided that tonight would be the perfect time to remedy that situation.

Fortified with several glasses of wine for courage, we wound up in a godforsaken part of the city at a hellhole dive called The Pink Poodle. As we approached the door, she in her gold lamé evening gown and I in my tuxedo, were asked by the doorman if we were sure we knew what kind of place it was.

"It's a tit bar, isn't it? And we've never been to one," she replied. Once inside, we found a café table away from the stage against a wall. We ordered wine. It was served in plastic cups and tasted as if it had come from the reduced-for-quick-sale bin at the 7-Eleven convenience store. On the table was a half-empty wicker basket with a mixture of pretzels and peanuts. Not knowing how long it had been sitting there or whose hands had been in it, we declined to partake.

Looking around the dimly lit room, we noticed that there were strands of multicolored Christmas lights hanging on the walls and a small stage with two dance poles. The club was about half full of drunken sailors drooling over two dancers fifteen years too old and twenty pounds too heavy to still be prancing around the stage in their G-strings and pasties (which appeared to have been purchased at Kmart).

We stayed long enough to finish our wine, laughing ourselves silly at the scene playing out before us. We have not been back since.

Hermeine Tovey, dressed in her gold lame, and I in my tux.
Bailey collection

Cucumbers and Christmas Carols

In December of 1990, the Piggly Wiggly decided to put a piano in one of their flagship stores the week leading up to Christmas. The store, located between two major highways and adjacent to the Citadel Mall, was guaranteed high foot traffic.

A mid-sized, black Yamaha grand was delivered, tuned and placed between the checkout lanes and the produce department. Beginning December 18 and running until the store closed on Christmas Eve, there was to be live holiday music from noon until 8pm. The seven days were divided into two four-hour shifts per day among seven local pianists. Each covered two shifts over the course of the week. Greg Jones, Hermeine Tovey, JoAnn Killingworth, Benjy Haywood, Ricky Duckett, Kathy Sloan, and I were the featured performers. I was assigned two of the second shifts, which were from four in the afternoon until eight in the evening. This, being the busiest time of day, was perfect.

The store was appropriately decorated for the season in a manner conducive to luring shoppers into impulsive purchases. Large displays of baking ingredients and decorations were strategically placed near a table of fully assembled gingerbread houses and kits and prebaked Christmas cookies. Each checkout lane had displays of peppermint candy canes and assorted boxed chocolates to tempt children and last minute shoppers. The entry to each aisle was swaged with artificial holly garland. Atop the piano was a large poinsettia, its pot wrapped in bright red floral foil and a large green and white, handtied satin bow. A fishbowl encircled in silver tinsel garland sat on the side of the music rack with a hand drawn placard featuring holly leaves on each of its four corners sported the word "TIPS" written in alternating red and green ink. The store staff donned black pants, white shirts, and red and green vests with their employee nametags pinned to them. Each wore a little elf cap with a small bell at the point.

My first shift came early in the week and was rather routine. The second and final performance was December 23rd. By this time, every store in town was packed with people making final purchases for their holiday celebrations. There was an energy in the air not unlike static electricity. A sense of urgency, excitement, anticipation, and frustration seemed to permeate the general atmosphere.

Seated at the piano, the surroundings suggested *It's Beginning to Look A Lot like Christmas* for my opening song. Several shoppers stopped by the piano to talk, and most of them put tips in the fishbowl. The constantly changing clientele provided abundant people-watching opportunities.

There were old ladies in tailored suits with droopy stockings and blue or purple rinses on their freshly coiffed heads. Soccer moms in their ugly Christmas sweaters chased after their unruly children. Businessmen on their way home from their offices wandered aimlessly up and down the aisles attempting to find the items their wives had forgotten earlier in the day. I put my hands on automatic pilot and enjoyed the show unfolding before me.

Somewhere between *God Rest Ye Merry Gentlemen* and *What Child is This?* I noticed two police officers enter the store and move down separate aisles. Shortly thereafter, they led a disheveled looking person out of the store in handcuffs. Upon concluding that the incident was a foiled attempt at a little Christmas shoplifting, I segued into a medley of *Jailhouse Rock* and *Folsom Prison Blues.*

As the afternoon melted into evening, the store got busier. Half dozen children ran around as their mothers, seemingly oblivious to their antics, shopped. Something streaked past me. A little boy who appeared to be about six years old was chasing another little boy. Above the music came a female voice I assumed to be the mother of the two future Olympic sprinters, shouting for them to stop running. Paying her no attention, one of them found a box of instant mashed potato flakes. He opened it and gleefully threw fistfuls of it into the air, proclaiming it was snowing. I took that as a not-so-subtle cue to play *Let it Snow* and *Frosty the Snowman.*

"Cleanup on aisle two!" crackled over the store public address system. A bagboy appeared with a broom and dustpan. The woman, who had been bellowing from across the store moments earlier for her children to stop running, was now dragging the miscreants out of the store, leaving her shopping unfinished. She swatted their bottoms every few steps.

A calmer encounter arose when an older lady in her mid-70's has complimented my playing and asked me if I knew "Star of the East." She said it was a childhood favorite but she seldom heard it anymore. I played it a couple of times through for her. She thanked me for the trip down memory lane, wished me Merry Christmas, and put some cash in the bowl.

It is funny how one song can suggest others; the previously requested song made me think of *Star of Bethlehem* from the movie "Home Alone." As I played, the children remaining in the store recognized the song and gathered around the piano. When I finished, they each shared with me their favorite parts or lines from the film. I asked them what their favorite songs were and played each one. *The Chipmunk Song, Rudolph the Red-Nosed Reindeer, Grandma Got Run Over By a Reindeer, Up on the Housetop, Santa Claus is Coming to Town, All I Want For Christmas is my Two Front Teeth, I Want a Hippopotamus for Christmas,* and the song from the cartoon *How the Grinch Stole Christmas* kept them entertained for about twenty minutes.

One by one, their parents came to collect them, leaving me a nice tip in appreciation for babysitting while they finished their shopping.

The last to leave was a little girl about seven years old. She told me her name was Chloe and I had not played *her* favorite Christmas song. I asked her what it was. She replied that she didn't know, but it was on the Charlie Brown Christmas Special that she had watched with her grandmother the night before. I told her that I had watched that show every single Christmas since it came out in 1965 and knew all the songs from it. I started playing *Linus and Lucy*.

"That's not it!" she exclaimed. Next, I tried *Hark! The Herald Angels Sing*.

"Nope," she said, "wrong one."

Could she have meant Beethoven's *Fur Elise*? I got about the first two measures played before she told me that still wasn't the one. Out of ideas, I asked her when in the show the song comes on.

"At the beginning when it's first coming on and it's snowing and they're all ice skating," she said. Her face lit up as brightly as the fluorescent lights above us as I started the opening notes to *Christmas Time is Here*.

"That's it! That's it!" she shouted. Her grandmother came to the piano, and when the song ended, she told me she hoped Chloe wasn't annoying me. I assured her that she wasn't and that we had been having a ball playing "Name That Tune." They wished me the best the season had to offer and wheeled their shopping cart toward the checkout lanes.

Jingle, jingle, jingle, jingle came the sound of the little bells on two store employees' caps as they passed the piano.

"I hate these hats. They're hot and they make my scalp itch", said one to the other.

Jingle, jingle, jingle. I launched into a medley of *Jingle Bells, Jingle Bell Rock, and Sleigh Ride.*

A new commotion then similarly lent itself to my musical narration.

"What do we need with all this food, Clara? It's just the two of us and maybe the Johnsons for Christmas Eve dinner. You've got enough stuff in that cart to feed the Russian army for a month!" a man barked impatiently at his wife.

I glanced over to observe a cart so laden with groceries that not even a toothpick would fit in it. I thought that if four people consumed that much food at one meal, they would be miserable the next day. Without even thinking, I started to play the Alka Seltzer commercial music – *Plop, Plop, Fizz, Fizz, Oh What a Relief it is.*

I was disrupted from my people watching when a produce department employee approached me. He had been watching me most of the afternoon while stocking and restocking vegetables and gave the appearance of being slightly challenged. In his hand was a small cucumber. When he got about three feet from me, he looked at me lasciviously with the vegetable in hand and inquired about an obscene comparison.

"Get back to the storeroom, Eddie! You know you don't talk to customers or bother the piano players!" shouted the produce manager. As Eddie, cucumber in hand, scampered off and disappeared behind the swinging doors leading to the store stockroom, the manager of the department apologized. She explained that Eddie "wasn't right in the head" and was there for vocational training. I laughed.

I glanced at my watch. It was 7:53 pm, and I had seven minutes to play my closing medley of *"Have Yourself a Merry Little Christmas," "Happy Holidays,"* and *"We Wish You a Merry Christmas"*. About halfway through the medley, a homeless person grabbed the fishbowl (which was now filled to the brim with cash) and ran from the store. Security tackled him in the parking lot, causing the bowl to shatter on the asphalt. They managed to retrieve all of the money. The store manager presented me with a check for the two afternoons, a gift card as an apology for Eddie, and an invitation to play a return engagement in 1991.

Camelot

In late January of 1993, Camelot went into production at the James F. Dean Theatre in Summerville, South Carolina, home of the Flowertown Players. Pre-production was carried out in the usual way. The artistic director, musical director, and costumes, lighting, sound, and set designers met several times to plan the logistics of getting the production on stage the first three weeks of May. With the technical details ironed out, the arduous task of casting began. Auditions were advertised and held. After a series of callbacks, the principal roles were cast.

Kathy Sloan, the musical director of the production, was midway through a month-long run of *The Pirates of Penzance* with another theater company. It would be four to six weeks before she would be able to devote her undivided attention to the Camelot production. Kathy had been my high school organ teacher. In the two decades that had passed we remained friends. She continued to be a mentor. Her philosophy had been "versatility is employability." From early on, she had encouraged me to develop other musical skills than classical organ. It was during those high school years that she began teaching me piano styling and giving me opportunities to put my newly acquired techniques to practical use. She had me substitute for her on piano jobs when she was double-booked, sick, or just needed a night off. Now, the opportunity with which she was presenting me was the role of rehearsal pianist. For the first few weeks, my job was to work with the cast members on their solo numbers and the chorus on the group numbers. She came in on Saturday mornings for full cast music rehearsals. At these, she would play and I made notes about the passages she wanted the singers to work on until the next rehearsal with her. All went well. Most of the principals read music. John Kazee, who was portraying King Arthur, held advanced degrees in both voice and opera production. He was a blessing to me. I played the songs and beat out notes and rhythms for the cast members who were struggling while he worked on fine-tuning the choral ensemble.

By early March, Pirates had wrapped and Kathy was free to be at the remainder of the Camelot rehearsals. My job was completed.

The final rehearsals went well. The Wednesday before Friday's opening night, Kathy and John appeared on a midday talk show to promote the production. They performed *How to Handle a Woman*, one of his solo numbers. That evening, the entire cast videotaped the show in the empty theater for critique purposes. The following evening, family and friends of the cast were welcomed at the dress rehearsal. Opening night, the following night, and the Sunday matinee was sold out and huge successes. We were off to a great start and had high hopes for the next two weekends (which were also sold out). There was even talk about extending the production into a fourth weekend if the theater manager could work out an arrangement regarding royalties with the owners of the copyright in New York.

The second week did not go as well. Pollen season was at its peak. The entire town was blanketed in yellow dust. Several of the principal cast members were adversely affected and would have to perform under the influence of Benadryl and other anti-allergy medication to be able to get through the show without watery eyes and runny noses. A couple of them were having allergy-related vocal issues. Kathy did warm-ups with each singer prior to the evenings' performances, during which she determined what their best high and low notes were at that particular time. Once that had been established, she would then transpose their solo numbers into whatever key they could comfortably and accurately sing at the given moment. With the help of pharmaceuticals and a talented musical director who could easily transpose at sight, the crisis had been averted.

On the second night of the second week, disaster struck. The lighting crew in the tech booth cut the house lights before Kathy was seated at the piano. She took a misstep, fell, and broke her right elbow. Ever the professional, she played the entire show with a broken and rapidly swelling arm and then drove herself to the emergency room. She was put in a hard cast from her elbow to her wrist with her right thumb immobilized. The next morning, she called to relay the details of the previous evening and to ask me to come help her juggle music, turn pages, and double melody notes at the octave as needed that evening until she figured out how to play with her four exposed fingers. She did an excellent job rearranging accompaniments to accommodate her temporarily diminished ability to use her right hand. She did it with such skill that the quality of the music did not suffer. Between musical numbers, she rested her arm on a pillow in her lap. Deciding she could manage on her own from then on, I thought my job was finished.

They say things come in threes. In the case of our production, no truer statement had ever been uttered. Murphy's Law was in maximum overdrive. On Friday evening of the final weekend, Kathy asked me to come to the theater. She said her hand was bothering her and she would appreciate it if I would sit beside her on the bench, once again, turn pages, and pick up a note or chord here and there. I arrived at the theater about ten minutes before curtain time and took a seat beside her on the bench. The first act went well, requiring no assistance from me.

After intermission, I took a seat in a folding chair just left of the piano at the apron of the stage rather than returning to the piano bench. The second act began and was going beautifully. John and Nancyjean Smith were onstage in a long and emotional scene between King Arthur and Lady Guinevere. Just as the tension of the scene was reaching its climax, a voice sounded from the back of the theater.

"Is there a Mr. Vaughn Sloan here?" Kathy and I exchanged glances while John and Nancyjean continued the scene. About a minute later, the same voice, this time louder and more insistent, interrupted again.

"Mr. Vaughn Sloan, please report to the lobby."

"Who is that and what do they want with Vaughn?" Kathy whispered. I shrugged my shoulders. The scene onstage continued. Now, for the third time, the same voice rang out, "Vaughn Sloan to the lobby immediately."

Steve Jackson, helping backstage, exited the stage door and walked around to the front of the theater to see who was creating the disturbance and why. It was two Summerville Police officers who were there to tell Vaughn that his house had been broken into and he would have to accompany them home to file a report and list any items that may have been stolen. Steve explained to them that Mr. Sloan was at work but Mrs. Sloan was on the piano bench directing the show. They marched down the center aisle to the piano, told her what was happening at her residence, and explained that she needed to accompany them right away. She protested, explaining that the show had about forty more minutes to run and she would meet them there as soon as it was over. They insisted she go with them. They lifted her from the piano bench, escorting her from the theater via the fire exit. As she departed, she told me, "You'll have to finish tonight's performance."

Waves of panic swept over me as I slid onto the piano bench. Looking up onto the stage at John and Nancyjean, our eyes met, and an unspoken but collective *Oh, shit!* was telepathically communicated between the three of us. Steve apprised Terry Lee, a cast member who was in charge of the chorus when not on stage, of the situation. As the news circulated, all hell broke loose backstage in the dressing rooms. By the time word had reached everyone behind the scenes, the story was that a house was being robbed and they had taken Kathy. Imaginations ran wild, and backstage cast and crew were thinking a band of marauders had entered the theater, were robbing patrons at gunpoint, and holding Kathy hostage. John and Nancyjean finished the scene and exited the stage as the character Mordred entered to sing *The Seven Deadly Virtues*. At that point, there was more adrenaline pumping through my body than blood. My heart rate and pulse were elevated, and my breathing was rapid. It was sink or swim. Placing my hands on the keys, I started the introduction to the song. I seemed to be playing at twice the tempo, but the actor on stage stayed with me. Trying as I might to contain my anxiety, I was becoming more nervous with each passing minute.

The big scene in which Lady Guinevere is marched to the stake to be burned was quickly approaching. The way in which this scene had been blocked called for the actors to come down the center aisle escorting Guinevere. While this was occurring, the chorus positioned onstage was to sing a dirge describing the action-taking place. The tempo of the piece was meant to be somber and slow in the style of a funeral march. It didn't quite happen that way at this particular performance.

Adrenaline still pumping and my nerves on edge, I tore through the music like an Oktoberfest polka. I knew it was entirely too fast but was powerless to do anything about it. I prayed that the singers would slow down; forcing me to follow them, but that was not to be. The faster I played, the faster they sang. Mercifully, the actor portraying Sir Lancelot took to the stage right on cue and rescued Lady Guinevere, thus ending the scene with its runaway musical accompaniment.

The play ended 15 minutes later. The curtain call followed the usual protocol: Smaller parts and extras first, then principals in order of character stature. John and Nancyjean were the last actors called to the stage for bows. Next, the cast acknowledged the tech crew. When all had taken their bows, the cast reprised the last two lines of the title song, "Camelot." At the conclusion of the song, the entire assembly turned toward me, extending their arms and motioned for me to stand. I was not prepared for what followed—the entire audience gave a standing ovation lasting over three minutes. I was paralyzed. I couldn't bow; sit back down, wave, or anything. I was frozen. Never before had I been shown so much appreciation, especially for what I considered to be the worst performance I had ever given. At the cast party, Craig Stanley, the actor who brilliantly portrayed Merlin, read the following ballad that he composed, lampooning that fateful evening.

Sit close and I will unfold to thee
The tale of a Camelot tragedy.
It began when too quickly the lights went low
And Kathy went tumbling down below.
Like a trooper she managed to play right through.
But a broken elbow would call its due.
In the morning a search went out through the land.
But alas, poor Kathy would play with one hand.
But alas, poor Kathy would play with one hand.
But alas, poor Kathy would play with one hand

Then places were called on that Saturday night
And all the players were filled with fright
It was going remarkably well that day
Then Summerville's finest took Kathy away.
Then Tom, a stranger to this score
With fear in his eyes looked for a door
But the doors were blocked and the stage was set.
When Lance started singing, he tried his best.
When Lance started singing, he tried his best.
When Lance started singing, he tried his best.

Then Terry came to this balladeer
and said that Kathy was no longer here.
The house is being robbed right now.
I looked around and wondered how.
"So we have no music" I seemed to say.
She said, "Tom Bailey will try to play."
He will bring us through with a lot of luck
For he doesn't know the music cuts.
For he doesn't know the music cuts.
For he doesn't know the music cuts.

Tom played and faked with the rest of us
And we never heard a word or fuss.
In the back, Steve Jackson was pulling his hair
Knowing Tom was wishing that he wasn't there.
The cast was pale with a look of fear
Knowing soon would be time to sing "Guinevere"
We wondered what the key would be
I started singing in one of three
I started singing in one of three
I started singing in one of three.

The opening of solo of "Guinevere"
Was a torment to the listener's ear.
The tale was told like skinning a cat
So thankful I was behind the flat.
Tom played a merry burning tune
Like something we do in the land every June.
With cheer in our voice Jenny went to the stake
While Arthur and Mordred pretended to fake.

While Arthur and Mordred pretended to fake.
While Arthur and Mordred pretended to fake.

The cast and crew of the show that night
Brought an end to this ill-fated turkey's flight.
Through the grace of God and the efforts of all
We mounted the stage for our curtain call.
As we made our bows and our curtsies too
We anticipated an audience boo.
But the crowd was cheerful and proved a lot
They never knew cops were in Camelot
This once was a place known as Camelot.
This once was a place known as Camelot

Craig Stanley –
May 22, 1993
"Merlin"

Nancyjean "Lady Guinevere" Nettles shared her impressions of the events of the evening for this book.

Until that night, the most nerve-wracking moments of playing Guinevere in Camelot were the times I spent sitting on a bench gazing at Lancelot while he sang "If Ever I would Leave You." It's a beautiful love song, which he sang gloriously, but poor Guinevere had nothing to do except gaze adoringly at Lance for what seemed like an eternity.

However, "nerve-wracking" was about to take on new meaning. Flickers of movement occurred just in front of the stage. Policemen appeared . . . whispered conversations took place as Lance sang . . . and then I glimpsed the officers escort Kathy up the aisle and out of the theater, as Tom Bailey slid over on the piano bench and began playing, not missing a note.

What in the world was going to happen with Kathy gone? How could Tom possibly know that the keys to ALL the songs for Arthur and me had been raised? A million nightmare possibilities were ricocheting within my head, especially the notion that Arthur and I would have to dance for an additional two minutes that Kathy had deleted from "What Do the Simple Folk Do?"

Amazingly, she had made notations on the score, and miraculously, Tom read them on the fly and managed every change. As frightened as we were on stage, Tom had to have been even more terrified than we were. I will never know how he managed to play so perfectly. And I'll always be grateful for his professionalism, as well as for the graciousness of the audience who gave all of us a standing ovation. As it turned out, instead of experiencing a nightmare we wanted to forget, we were given an incredibly memorable stage story with an exhilarating ending. The magic and adventure of live theater!

Nancyjean (Smith) Nettles

From the Mouths of Babes

In the 1960's, Art Linkletter had a television show called "Kids Say the Darndest Things." He later had some of the funnier moments from the show transcribed into a book of the same title. In my experience, as both a classroom music teacher and a private piano teacher, I have heard some wild things come out of the mouths of babes.

I answered my door one afternoon to find Paul, my seven-year-old piano student, standing on the top step. His music bag was in his hand, and he was crying uncontrollably. I asked him what was wrong and why he was crying. He tried to answer, but the words got lost between sobs. I brought him in the house and got a box of Kleenex so he could blow his nose and dry his eyes. I wet a washcloth with cool water, wrung it out, and put it on his face to cool him down. He finally stopped crying and told me that his older sister, who had driven him to his lesson, had spanked him with her sandal before getting in the car to come to my house.

"Why did she spank you?" I asked.

"I don't know," he replied.

I told him that he must have done something to warrant being punished. He insisted he had done nothing.

"Well, there must have been a good reason," I said.

"There is," he answered. "It's because she is a bitch!"

I had to leave the room so he wouldn't catch me laughing.

For twenty-five years, I taught general music classes to children in four-year-old kindergarten through fifth grade. One day, I was sitting in the library during my free period visiting with the librarian. There had been a story on the national news that week about a little boy in Arizona who had been bitten by a rattlesnake in the play area of a hamburger restaurant. Apparently, there was a slide that would take the children down into hundreds of multicolored sponge and plastic balls at the bottom. The snake had somehow gotten into the play area and was under the balls. When the little boy landed on it, he was bitten.

Andrew, a kindergartner, came up to the desk to check out a Dr. Seuss book.

"Guess what?" He said. "I'm not allowed to play on the slide when we go out to eat anymore. It's not safe. My mom saw on TV that a little boy was playing on the slide and a snake bit him in the balls."

Another incident at the same school involved a five-year-old flasher and her classmates. Melissa had discovered that little girls were different from little boys and was taking every opportunity to educate her classmates. I had been told by the classroom teacher that this was going on and the best way to handle it was simply to ignore it. She did it for attention more than anything else.

Several weeks passed and nothing happened. I had forgotten the entire conversation with my colleague. One day in the middle of a song, several students started calling my name at once.

"Mr. Bailey, Mr. Bailey!"

I stopped playing and singing to see what the trouble was.

"Melissa is showing us her private parts again," said Josh,

"No I'm not!" Melissa yelled at him.

"Yes, you are too!" Several little girls shouted.

"She does it all the time," said little Derek.

"No I don't either, you're a liar Derek!" Melissa hollered at him.

Envisioning the situation potentially getting out of hand, I suggested that everyone settle down and get back to our song.

A few minutes later, someone else said, "She's doing it again!"

"I am not," Melissa protested.

"Yes you are!" Said Laurie. "Mr. Bailey, she does this all the time; just ask our teacher! She even knows what you call it." "Yeah!" Said Johnny. "That's all we hear all day long—Virginia, Virginia, Virginia!"

Vegas, Baby

By the late summer of 2002, I had been playing the early part of the week at Charleston Chops for five years. I had become good friends with the owner, Judy Ballenger. We spent holidays together; she had seen me through the death of my father, a horrible bout of walking pneumonia, and various other life events. I had been with her through numerous staff turnovers, the hiring and firing of several weekend musicians, and the birth of her first two grandchildren.

After work, we would sit at the bar and, over a glass of wine, talk about things serious and silly. Neither of us ever worried about the other betraying confidences. The serious conversations were kept between us.

One night in early August, we were having our nightcap before leaving the restaurant when she told me she was orchestrating a wedding for the daughter of a close friend of hers. It was to be held at the Bellagio Hotel in Las Vegas on September 12. All of the details had been arranged and confirmed with the exception of a pianist for the ceremony.

"You wouldn't consider doing it for me, would you," she asked.

It took me about five seconds to agree unconditionally.

The wedding party left Charleston on the Sunday afternoon before the wedding. I remained in Charleston to cover my Monday and Tuesday night shift, having arranged for the weekend entertainer to cover Wednesday night. I was a little nervous about flying on September 11th. It was the one-year anniversary of the attacks on the World Trade Center. I had been in London, England and was due to return to the United States on September 12th. Thanks to Mr. Bin Laden, I had been trapped in the United Kingdom for another six days. There are worse places on the globe for one to be stranded than England, but the uncertainty of what was to come had been a harrowing experience.

When we arrived at the Charleston International Airport for the first leg of the trip, there was hardly anyone in the terminal. The check-in agent told us that people fearing a repeat of the previous year were avoiding air travel that day. Arriving in Charlotte, North Carolina to make the connecting flight to Nevada, the scene was much the same. The plane was only about a quarter full for the four-hour flight.

Relieved to have landed safely, we took a cab to the Bellagio and were settled in a room on the sixteenth floor. Due at a late afternoon cocktail reception in one of the banquet rooms in a few hours; I decided to take a nap. I was awakened around seven in the evening by the bedside telephone. On the other end of the line was one of the hotel wedding chapel coordinators who wanted to know what color piano I wanted and what brand. I could choose a Baldwin or a Yamaha in black, brown, or white. I told her the wedding was formal so the black grand would probably photograph the best.

Being assured that both brands were tuned weekly and kept in excellent repair, I chose the Yamaha and arranged to come play it the following morning.

At the appointed time, I met the coordinator at the hotel chapel where the piano had been brought for my approval. After about five minutes of scales, arpeggios, and progressions, I played a few of the pieces on the program for the evening. The piano was in fine tune with a medium action. I was neither too stiff nor too loose. Satisfied, I departed the chapel. Just outside the door, I was stopped by a man who introduced himself. His name was Dante. He complimented my playing and asked if I was one of the hotel pianists. I told him I was not, but would be playing a wedding later in the day. He relayed that he had been one of the stable of pianists employed by the hotel when it first opened but was now freelancing and working at the Liberace Museum playing during tours. He asked if I planned to visit the museum while in town. Telling him it was on my schedule later in the morning, he told me to come find him when I got there.

The cab ride from the hotel to the museum on the Tropicana Avenue took about ten minutes. The museum occupied a small strip shopping center. A sign in the shape of a grand piano alerted tourists to its location. Each building housed a different exhibit. There was a display of all of the cars Liberace drove as well as the ones used on stage. Another section displayed silver, china, crystal, and antique furniture culled from his various residences. In a separate building, a restaurant complete with a piano bar occupied another portion of the shopping center. The longest building housed the gift shop and the piano room where all of the pianos from his homes and the ones used on stage and in films was displayed. The Hall of Costumes was a large room, the walls lined with ceiling-to-floor mirrors. In the center of the room was a mirrored Baldwin grand used in the Las Vegas nightclub shows in which he headlined. Along the mirrored walls were life-sized mannequins wearing the various capes, tuxedos, and costumes for which "Mr. Showmanship" was famous.

I found Dante who introduced me to a docent. She gave me a personal guided tour. Once in the room with the pianos, she said Dante had told her to have me play any of them I wanted to. There were many to choose from, but I was drawn to a Baldwin grand covered in rhinestones. I played for about fifteen minutes. As I got up from the piano and replaced the velvet rope, Dante approached me.

"Hey, how would you like to play during a public tour tomorrow morning at eleven o'clock?" he asked. I accepted the invitation without hesitation. After making all of the arrangements, we returned to the hotel to prepare for the formal diner in one of the Bellagio restaurants. After dinner, the bridal couple and younger members of the wedding party went out to continue the celebration on the famous strip. The over-forty crowd, of which I was a member, retired to one of the penthouse suites for cocktails.

I hardly slept that night and was up early the next morning to prepare for my guest appearance at the museum. Upon my arrival, Dante escorted me to the Hall of Costumes so I could have some time with the piano before the tour group got there. At precisely eleven o'clock, the doors swept open and three-hundred chattering tourists from Germany entered the hall for the ten-minute portion of the tour. I played themes from Adinsell's *Warsaw Concerto* and Gershwin's *Rhapsody in Blue*. Having seen the costumes, the group adjourned to other parts of the museum, thus ending my performance. Descending the platform upon which the piano sat, it occurred to me what I had just done.

Never did I imagine that I would ever play in Las Vegas, let alone at two high-profile venues, one of which possessed one of the most famous pianos in show business. I seriously doubt that I could duplicate the experience. I had been at the right place at the right time with the right people.

Dante told me that if I ever wanted to relocate to Nevada, he would keep me busy at the museum playing tours. Returning to the Bellagio, the morning's events were recounted to Judy. I told her of the offer of employment. She said I was not leaving Charleston Chops until she did, and I didn't. I was with her until 2006 when Chops closed its doors. I have not been back to Las Vegas to play, for a wedding or a getaway since. Will I ever? Who knows—it was the experience of a lifetime.

Performing on Liberace's piano.

Bailey collection

The wedding party in Las Vegas.
Bailey collection

Publicity Photo
Bailey collection

Here Come the Brides

Weddings are a joy to some musicians and a vexation to others. Each bride has her own personality and her own vision of her special day. It does not matter if it is a first wedding or if she is making her fourth or fifth trip down the aisle; each one comes with a list of requirements to guarantee the perfect wedding day.

I have never been subjected to a "bridezilla". By the time, they get to me for their initial consultation, the wedding director at the church, the officiant, or the event planner has already dealt with problems, unreasonable demands, or meltdowns born from frustration or stress. Occasionally, a bride will have her heart set on a piece of music that does not transcribe well as a solo piano or organ piece. Once I play it for her at the consultation and she hears for herself that an acoustic piano or an organ cannot replicate a lead singer, backup singers, and a full rock band effectively, she quickly rethinks her choice of music and asks for suggestions. All things considered, the job of a wedding pianist or organist is easy in comparison to the other service providers working behind-the-scenes.

With any event in which many people are involved, mishaps are bound to occur. Some are easily fixed while others are beyond the control of anyone. In over forty years of providing music for these occasions, I have seen my share of things too unbelievable to be anything but true.

One Saturday around Thanksgiving, I was scheduled to play a large wedding at Saint Peter's by the Sea Episcopal Church. I had been the organist and the Director of Music there for about a year, and though I had already played several weddings, this was to be the largest to date. The church was located in a declining neighborhood one block from the main gate of the Navy base amid pawnshops, adult theaters and topless clubs. It was affectionately referred to as "Saint Peter's by the Strip."

The bride and groom were not members of the church but had roundabout, family connections to the parish. They were being married there because the Eternal Father of the Sea Chapel on the base already had three weddings scheduled.

The groom, a young, Navy ensign, and bride, a nurse at the Navy hospital, were delightful to work with and very appreciative of being allowed to use the church despite not being members. The reception was held back on the base at the officer's club, so the location was perfect.

The rehearsal went well, considering there were twelve bridesmaids and twelve groomsmen for whom to find a place on the small chancel (which also housed the choir pews, organ pipes, pulpit, and entrance to the altar).

All seemed well the afternoon of the ceremony. The key participants were on site an hour-and-a-half beforehand. The church sexton had dutifully hosed down all of the sidewalks to remove the calling cards of the pigeons and seagulls (who made daily visits to claim the breadcrumbs that Agnes, a parishioner, brought to put on the church lawn).

At 3:30 pm, I slid onto the organ bench to begin the prenuptial music. The church was about half-full. The first selection was a rather loud piece. Upon striking the first chord, I heard a flapping sound. Continuing to play, I looked up to see a pigeon perched atop the middle pipe in the organ case. The sound must have startled it. I had visions of it flying through the church dive-bombing the guests, but thankfully, it just sat on that organ pipe.

The wedding began. The attendants all processed in and took their places on the chancel in the choir pews. The bride made a spectacular entrance. The ceremony continued. The priest reached the part of the ceremony in which he propositioned "If anyone can show just cause why these two should not be lawfully married, speak now or forever hold his peace." In response, a young woman leapt to her feet, and in a thick accent, declared, "He mine. I find in bar. She not have him. He mine!"

The ceremony stopped, and the woman was escorted to the sacristy where the priest heard her out, decided her objection had no legal or moral validity, and sent her tearfully on her way.

It seemed that after the bachelor party, the groom and some of his friends had gone to a bar near the base. The woman was in the bar and tried in vain to pick him up. He had firmly but gently rebuffed her advances, but had told her she was a pretty girl and that she would find someone. He then made the mistake of kissing her on the cheek. In her culture, a kiss was as good as a promise of marriage.

The ceremony continued, the pronouncement of marriage was made, and the couple departed the church under crossed swords. As the wedding party began exiting the chancel and processing down the center aisle, a scream was heard above the organ music. My first thought was that the woman who had been sent away had attacked the bride on the sidewalk. I quickly glanced around to see what was going on. A bridesmaid, still in the choir pews waiting her turn to exit the church, was tugging frantically at the front of her dress. The pigeon that had been clinging to the organ pipe throughout the wedding had died, fallen forward, and landed in the front of her strapless, loose-fitting gown. She left the church by way of sacristy. The pigeon was removed.

Playing for outdoor nuptials is always a challenge. It is difficult to play with any degree of artistry while swatting gnats, holding down the music the wind is determined to carry away (despite the pins that are supposed to hold it in place), and squinting at the blinding sun. I try not to accept these engagements, but some are unavoidable. Such was the case of a spring ceremony to be held in the wedding garden at the Charles Towne Landing State Park. The garden, most easily accessible by tram, is located in the middle of the park in an enclosure of azalea bushes with a lush, sloping lawn that ends at a large pond.

The day of the ceremony was perfect. There was not a cloud in the sky, the temperature was hovering between 78 and 80 degrees, and a steady but gentle breeze kept the guests cool and the gnats at bay (but lacked the strength to send the music flying or cause vacant folding chairs to tip). The ceremony was traditional and the wedding party small.

The officiant was speaking when I noticed the guests begin to get restless in their seats. I looked back but could not see anything. I thought perhaps some of the folding chairs had been positioned over an ant bed. A few minutes passed, and a few of the guests got up from their chairs. The bride, groom, best man, and maid of honor each did a little sidestep and started slowly making their way toward the assembled guests. I still had no idea what was happening. Positioned behind the rows of folding chairs, I could only see the backs of the guests and the wedding party.

As soon as the officiant pronounced the couple husband and wife, I started the recessional music. The couple and the attendants made a hasty retreat to the tram, followed by the officiant and the guests. It was not until then that I realized what was causing the anxiety. A rather large alligator had come out of the pond onto the lawn and was sunning itself just a few feet away from where the vows were being exchanged.

As I was finishing the Purcell piece, the rogue reptile slowly moved up the lawn. Fats Waller had a song called *Alligator Crawl*, a boogie-woogie tune popular in the 1940's. I briefly entertained the idea of playing part of it for comic relief. However, the animal was gaining speed in its trek up the lawn. Since the keyboard belonged to the office at the park and was set up and taken down by the staff, I thought it best to quickly gather my music and join the others on the tram back to more civilized parts of the park.

It was a rainy New Year's Eve when I arrived at a church along a frontage road parallel to the interstate to provide the piano music for a 6 pm ceremony. The call requesting my services had come earlier in the afternoon. Already booked to play for a party at the private residence from 8 pm until midnight, I accepted the extra job. I would simply leave home three hours earlier than originally planned. The church was not at all out of my way.

The mother of the bride said to play traditional wedding music. I arrived at 5 pm and introduced myself to a lady from the church who was the volunteer wedding coordinator. She showed me to the piano where I began unpacking my briefcase. Just as I was, about to sit down at the piano and run a few scales to get a feel for the action, in walked my pianist friend, Michele Russell. I asked if she was a friend of the bride or groom. She didn't know either of them; the mother of the bride had called her to engage her services the day before. We both were a little embarrassed. I told her that since she had been asked the day before, that she should play, explaining that I already had a job for the evening, anyway. As I began putting away my music, yet another pianist arrived. All three of us were totally perplexed. How could a situation like this have happened? The third pianist was a little miffed because he had not wanted the job in the first place. He felt sorry for the bride's mother; she had called him three hours earlier and begged him to come so that there would be music for her daughter's wedding day. Totally confused and a bit annoyed, we asked to see the bride's mother. She appeared from the back. After introductions were made, we asked why she had booked three pianists and which one she wanted to stay. She said that her eldest daughter had been married three years earlier and that the musician never came. She booked three for this one, thinking that at least one would come. She said it did not matter to her, which one of us stayed. The last pianist to arrive had not wanted to be there anyway, and I was already booked later in the evening. We decided that Michele should stay. It would have been nice had we all three been paid, but needless to say that did not happen.

Saint Luke's Chapel on the campus of the Medical University of South Carolina is a venue where I play twenty or more weddings annually. Since it is a building for hire, not associated with any religion or denomination, the weddings held there run the gamut from very traditional to you-wouldn't-believe-it-without-seeing-it-for-yourself.

One memorable ceremony was for a middle-aged couple. They had been together for over a decade and decided it was time to make it official. Both had been married in the past but neither had children. The ceremony was to be short and there would be about thirty guests.

The couple had an older Golden Retriever and wanted the dog included in the wedding party. About five minutes prior to the beginning of the ceremony, the matron of honor brought the dog onto the chancel and removed its leash. The procession to the altar took about a minute and the ceremony began.

In the chapel, the organ is positioned in such a way that the organists' back is to the chancel. There is no way to see what is happening. Halfway through the ceremony, I heard muffled laughter. Thinking perhaps a trickster had written "Help Me" on the bottom of the bride or groom's shoes or committed some other prank common at weddings, I thought no more about it. About a minute later, the entire congregation began laughing. My curiosity having gotten the better of me, I flipped around on the bench to see what was happening. The dog had left a wedding present in the middle of the chancel. Horrified, the bride chastised the dog, which, with its tail tucked between its legs, hid under the altar chair for the remainder of the ceremony.

Wedding receptions can be as unpredictable as the ceremonies that precede them. I like these functions because

I am usually sequestered in a corner, playing background music for people who aren't listening. The noise level is high, which affords me the opportunity to try out new music. If the piece doesn't go well, no one hears it anyway. Receptions are also great opportunities to indulge in my second passion: people watching. The average reception is an optical smorgasbord. One sees a parade of diverse people, all of whom have their own ideas about etiquette and decorum.

One memorable reception was held in a beautiful, historic mansion. The wedding would take place in the formal garden, and then everyone would ascend the staircase up to the piazza that ran the length of the house. Cocktails would be served and a formal dinner would follow.

As per my custom, I arrived about an hour prior to the time I was to start. The music for the ceremony was being provided by my friend Peter Kiral and his string ensemble. I wanted to hear as much of the music as I could. Once set up, I went into the dining room. From that vantage point, I would not only be able to hear the music but also watch the ceremony.

To say this group was not the classiest for whom I've ever played would be putting it mildly. They gave the appearance of being long on money, short on taste. Rodney Dangerfield's character in "Caddyshack" immediately came to mind. The bridesmaids were in white dresses with black dots. They looked more like actors in a production of 101

Dalmatians than attendants in a lovely southern garden wedding. The groomsmen looked like nerdy students from MIT or Cal. Tech in the 1950's. They donned black pants with oxford shoes, white shirts with red, plaid bowties, crewcuts and black, plastic-framed glasses. The only things missing were plastic pocket protectors.

The hour of the wedding arrived. Peter's string quartet started playing Pachelbel's *Canon in D*. I noticed that the first bridesmaid had started down the stairs towards the garden before the bride's mother had been seated. Often, both parents escort the bride to the altar, so I did not think much about it.

As the last attendant made her entrance, I heard an argument from the room across the foyer. The bride and her mother were having a heated discussion that quickly degenerated into a shouting match. The two women shrieked at each other like banshees. They were using language that would embarrass a sailor.

The problem, as it happened, was that the bride had sprained her foot, and the shoes for which she had paid $400 on sale would not fit. Her mother, yelling at her to get down the steps or she would drag her down them, was recounting the cost of the venue, the food, the music, the liquor, all of which totaled $30,000. The house manager offered a compromise, observing the situation and having an appreciation of the positions of both the bride and her mother. I was impressed with the diplomacy with which she diffused the situation. She suggested that since the bride was wearing a long dress and her feet would be unseen, she should consider not wearing shoes at the ceremony. She told her that it would be a shame to have the heels of such expensive shoes digging into the grass and being ruined. She suggested that by the time, the ceremony ended and everyone was upstairs seated, the swelling would have subsided and she could put the shoes on and wear them when they were visible and could be admired. Seeing the logic in her reasoning, the procession continued. I played for an hour and a half during the cocktail hour portion of the reception and went home. Peter made it to his next gig but just barely.

When too much alcohol is consumed, people who normally are very proper can become scandalous. Such was the case at a country club reception for which I played three decades ago. I was engaged to play the piano during the cocktail hour and dinner portion of the evening, after which a band called the Blue Notes, would perform for after-dinner dancing. The guest list was a veritable "who's who" from the world of business, industry, and society. There must have been 300 people there. The crowd was as coruscating as the jewels they wore and the cars in which they arrived.

One of the guests, a celebrated gentleman for whom buildings, roadways, scholarship funds, and foundations had been named, arrived with his second wife on his arm. Unlike his first wife, the epitome of who one would expect a man of his stature to be married to, this woman was loud, brassy, and usually drunk. Accompanying them was another couple. The wife ran a successful downtown business while her husband enjoyed the fruits of her labor.

Seated at a table near the piano, they drank heavily, hardly touching their dinner. The celebrated gentleman deposited a five-dollar bill on the piano and requested that I play *Mame*. He said it was his wife's favorite song and that they would like to dance to it. Both couples got up and began dancing. Shortly thereafter, all four were in a pile on the floor laughing hysterically. Legs had become entangled, causing all four people to trip.

Suddenly, the wife of the celebrity announced, "We have to go home. I've had an accident."

" What sort of accident?" Asked her husband.

"I've wet my pants," she answered.

He began feeling around on the carpet until he found the puddle.

"Wet your pants my ass," he exploded, "you pissed on the floor! How dare you embarrass me like this in public?"

Pulling her up from the floor, they left the club. A few months later, they resurfaced as though nothing had happened.

I was visiting my mother one weekend. It was one of those rare occasions when I just took a few days off to recharge my batteries. Mama was an accomplished musician and in demand as both a pianist and organist for a variety of functions. On this particular weekend, she was scheduled to play for the wedding of the son of one of her college friends. The ceremony was being held at the large United Methodist Church at which she was employed.

When she told me what she was playing, I decided to go with her to hear the music. Joyce Jones, Diane Bish, and the late Virgil Fox are the only organists whose performances of *Toccata* from Organ Symphony #5 by Widor can match my mothers. I play it, but she performed it.

Blue was the theme color of the wedding. The altar flowers and corsages were blue. The bridesmaids wore royal blue dresses and the groomsmen powder blue tuxedos. Even the mothers of the bride and groom wore dresses of different hues of blue.

The wedding was typical. The thirty-minute prelude was glorious. It is always a treat to hear another musician play, but it was especially a joy when it was my mother who, on a bad day, was ten times better than I am on my best day. I waited in the back of the church until the last F major chord ended *Toccata*. After she closed up the organ and set up her music for the next day's church service, we adjourned to the activities room for the reception. Mama usually did not attend receptions following weddings since she rarely had any connection to the couples and had not been invited. This was a bit different, as she knew the couple and the groom's parents.

Being the last to leave the church, we were at the back of the receiving line. Slowly making our way forward, we noticed that the blue theme had been carried over into the reception. There were several arrangements of blue flowers.

The skirting on the food tables was accented in blue, and the pen with which to sign the guestbook ad a blue feather plume. The wedding cake was white but had blue borders and was on a round table covered with a blue, sparkly material.

"Is this a wedding reception or a kid's Smurfs party?" I asked.

"Hush," Mama replied.

As we got closer to the food table, we were relieved to see that it was free of anything blue. Just as we were about to reach the wedding party to offer our congratulations, Mama handed me four quarters. I asked what the coins were for. "Look at the punch fountain."

Bubbling up and over the sides of the fountain into a large, crystal punch bowl was a bright blue liquid. The caterer had put blue food coloring in the punch.

"Go over to the machine in the back and get us two Diet Cokes," she said. "I draw the line at blue punch. I am not drinking anything that looks like Tidy Bowl."

***

Over my long career in music, I witnessed countless encounters like those described in these previous pages. I hope you enjoyed reading about them, as much as I enjoyed sharing them with you.

Tom Bailey

Acknowledgements

Ann Bailey: Typist, editor

Carole Brier: Technical advice

Hermeine Tovey: Cover artist, caricature of Betty

Cameron Hinkle: Artist photo

Charles Fox and David Vail: Use of Steinway Gallery of Charleston for photoshoot

Robin Meloy Gadsby, Robin Spielberg, and Dan Asher: Fellow pianists whose memoirs inspired me to put my own stories in print.

About the Author

Thomas W. Bailey Jr., a native of the South Carolina Lowcountry, has been performing continuously in the area since 1975. Although Charleston is his performance venue of choice, he has made guest appearances in New York City, San Antonio, Texas, Charlotte, North Carolina, Asheville, North Carolina, St. Augustine, Florida, Las Vegas, Nevada, and London, England.

Mr. Bailey has performed for three South Carolina governors and has appeared on stage with Hollywood celebrities Gary Collins and Mary Ann Mobley. In addition to his work as a pianist, he maintains an active career as a classical organist. He performed solo organ recitals for seven consecutive years (1986-1992) at the Piccolo Spoleto Festival in Charleston, South Carolina, and has given numerous recitals under the auspices of The American Guild of Organists. Currently, he performs at the piano weekly at the Francis Marion Hotel, the Charleston Place Belmond Hotel, and the Renaissance Charleston Historic District Hotel, all in downtown Charleston. Additionally, he is the organist and Director of Music at St. Theresa the Little Flower Catholic Church in Summerville, South Carolina, where he oversees the entire music program and is the founder and coordinator of the Third Sunday at Three concert series. He is retired from the parochial school system, having taught general music classes to kindergarten through fifth grade for twenty-five years. On top of a heavy performance schedule, he also teaches private piano and organ lessons in his home studio and is the coordinator for the Tuesday Noon Concert Series at St. Luke's Chapel on the campus of the Medical University of South Carolina in Charleston.

Thomas Bailey, 2016
Photo by Cameron Hinkle of
Rink Fine-Art Wedding and Lifestyle Portraiture

Made in the USA
Columbia, SC
29 July 2020